40 Descartes: Discours de la Méthode

Critical Guides to French Texts

EDITED BY ROGER LITTLE, WOLFGANG VAN EMDEN, DAVID WILLIAMS

DESCARTES

Discours de la Méthode

David Curtis

Lecturer in French
University of Hull

Grant & Cutler Ltd
1984

© Grant & Cutler Ltd
1984
ISBN 0 7293 0196 6

I.S.B.N. 84-490-7380-5

DEPÓSITO LEGAL: V. 1.560 - 1984

Printed in Spain by
Artes Gráficas Soler, S.A., Valencia
for
GRANT & CUTLER LTD
11 BUCKINGHAM STREET, LONDON W.C.2

Contents

Prefatory Note

The *Discours de la Méthode* has been consulted in the Nouveaux Classiques Larousse edition (Paris, 1972). Descartes's other works have been consulted in the C. Adam-P.Tannery edition available to me (Paris, Cerf, 1897-1913); this has been augmented, corrected and republished, Paris, Vrin, 1964-75. The *Regulae ad directionem ingenii* (Rules for the direction of the mind) have been quoted in J. Sirven's French translation (Paris, Vrin, 1970) which gives the Adam-Tannery pagination. Burman's Latin account of Descartes's conversation with him in 1648 has been consulted in J. Cottingham's English translation (Oxford, Clarendon Press, 1976).

References to the *Discours* are normally given thus: 2,7: 197-200 = Part 2, paragraph 7, lines 197 to 200. For ease of reference, 2,7 is taken to cover all four rules of Descartes's method, which is usually referred to simply as the Method. All other references are to the numbered items in the Bibliographical Note and are given thus: *1*, X, pp.400-01. *1* and *2* are respectively the numbers of Descartes's works and of Burman's account.

Finally, I take this opportunity to acknowledge the invaluable advice of my editors, especially of Professor David Williams.

Introduction

My aim in this book is to provide a necessarily short introduction to the *Discours* for non-specialists. I write as an historian of ideas attempting to understand the genesis and meaning of the *Discours*, to grasp in their historical context Descartes's intentions and the expectations of his readers. I do not write as a philosopher attempting a 'rational reconstruction of Descartes's thought' (*39*, p.10) or engaging in a critique of this thought from a particular point of view or from the viewpoints of later thinkers. Nor do I write as an historian of philosophy attempting to situate Cartesianism in the stream of Western philosophical thought. Where it appears to me that Descartes has not explained his views adequately I say so, and I try to give the reader some idea of the historical importance of the ideas depicted in the *Discours* and therefore, to some extent, of the ways in which these ideas have been challenged or even superseded. But my main concern is to reveal the presuppositions of the views expressed in the *Discours* and to elucidate the arguments Descartes puts forward to establish them. Readers will of course question both presuppositions and arguments for themselves, assisted by the works listed in the Bibliographical Note.

In conformity with the aim of this book and with the spirit of the *Discours* and of Cartesian philosophy as a whole I have used few technical terms; those asterisked are to be found in the short Glossary that precedes the Bibliographical Note. I have also, as far as possible, allowed Descartes to speak for himself, making many references to his other works. If the *Discours* is to function as a way into Descartes's thought as a whole, these references are worth following up with the help of Gilson's excellent commentary and of two key studies by Beck (*7*, *14* and *15*).

Again, I have respected as far as possible Descartes's own

order of presentation. Thus, having looked in Chapter 1 at the nature of the *Discours* and at the way in which it depicts Descartes's views, I examine in Chapter 2 the contents of Parts 1 and 2, in Chapter 3 those of Part 3 (with extensive reference to Part 6), in Chapter 4 those of Part 4, and in Chapter 5 those of Parts 5 and 6. The straightforward plan of my book is designed also to assist readers as they make their way through the *Discours*, enabling them, if they so wish, to read about a particular part before reading that part itself.

Finally, I have tried to respect the heterogeneous nature of the *Discours* and to cater for the needs of a non-specialist readership by adapting my approach in each chapter to the nature of the part(s) discussed therein. Thus, to give one example, I discuss at some length the stages of Descartes's *metaphysics, but do not provide a detailed account of his physics.

1. The Discours *and the 'art de persuader'*

When Descartes claims that the principles of his science are so self-evident that to understand them is to believe them (6,6: 291-92) and that 'ceux qui ont le raisonnement le plus fort, et qui digèrent le mieux leurs pensées, afin de les rendre claires et intelligibles, peuvent toujours le mieux persuader ce qu'ils proposent, encore qu'ils ne parlassent que bas breton, et qu'ils n'eussent jamais appris de rhétorique' (1,9: 148-52), he expresses his fundamental belief that truth is its own rhetoric. To think clearly and distinctly is *ipso facto* to persuade oneself of the truth of what one thinks, and to write clearly is *ipso facto* to persuade others of that truth; 'franchise' (1,5: 72) disdains any artificial rhetoric.

The most common *idée reçue* about the *Discours* is that it exemplifies this belief. It was, one often hears, the order and clarity, the eloquent logic of the work, which not only persuaded many of the truth of Descartes's ideas, but also contributed to the current literary evolution towards the Classicism of the 1660s and increased the prestige of the French language by discussing in it specialist subjects previously almost always treated in Latin.

There is of course some truth in this *idée reçue*; the effect it attributes to the *Discours* was real enough. But it does not do justice to the complex nature of the work. The *Discours* is not a work in which truth is its own rhetoric: it is not a work of unadulterated *clarté*. It is not an embodiment of Cartesianism, understood as a system that held naturalness, facility, simplicity and clarity to be both philosophical and aesthetic ideals and of which the essential order is the 'ordre des raisons' (*1*, III, p.266), a purely logical order: the nature of the *Discours* cannot be deduced from that of Cartesianism. On the contrary, the *Discours* is self-confessedly a 'tableau' (1,4: 57; 5,2: 33) with areas of light and shade (5,2: 31-36), a work of *clair/obscur* that aims to show rather than to demonstrate, to speak of Cartesian method rather than to teach it, to depict a man and his intellectual history rather than to recount a life or to expound a system. It is a work which is intentionally incomplete and, on occasions, intentionally ambiguous or vague: it is a work sometimes to be read between the lines.

Nor, paradoxically, does this *idée reçue* do justice to the extent of Descartes's redactional achievement. In this chapter I shall argue that this achievement was twofold: firstly, to have understood why only a work like the *Discours*, that is to say one in which truth could not be its own rhetoric, could and should be written; and secondly, to have employed more oblique and, paradoxically, more effective ways — what I have called his 'art de persuader' — of conveying his views. In order to appreciate the first point, we must look briefly at Descartes's purpose and temperament, the conditions under which he had to work, and the intellectual climate of Western Europe in his times.

Descartes was a man inspired by what he believed to be his mission to reform the whole of philosophy and science. He wished to break what he and other Catholic intellectuals such as Mersenne saw as the stranglehold of an outdated *Aristotelian philosophy upon the Christian faith and to replace Aristotelian natural philosophy with one that would be more useful to humanity. In a word, he wished to found a new Christian humanism, to be the new philosopher of the Catholic Church and the philosopher of the seventeenth-century Scientific Revolution.

However, this audacious and indeed impulsive man was also the most prudent of reformers. He knew from his own experience that he continually had to watch that his views did not appear to some to be paradoxical, to many to be dangerous novelty, to others again, and these were the most dangerous to his cause, to be but an echo of their own preconceptions (6,6: 253-59). He had, above all, to elicit favourable reactions from Church and State. He knew that his scientific work could be greatly helped by subvention from the State, at that time a supporter of the Church in its opposition to intellectual innovation, and that his reform could not succeed without

Church support, at that time unforthcoming. In 1633, on hearing of the condemnation in Rome of Galileo for putting forward Copernican *heliocentrism, he had prudently abandoned his plans to publish his ambitious general physics, *Le Monde*, which assumed the truth of heliocentrism. Four years later, Descartes could still not reveal the principles of his physics or openly support Galileo's opinion (6,1: 1-17) until the Inquisition's condemnation was revoked as he was confident it would be eventually. What could be done in the meantime?

Descartes's decision was characteristic of his unique combination of prudence and audacity. He would publish only samples of his work in order to gauge the strength of the present opposition to the publication of *Le Monde* and to persuade the public to help him overcome this opposition, which was hindering a reform intended to serve the public interest. Somehow he would find a way of appealing to widely differing tastes and abilities. He would seek to live up to the expectations of his friends, to intrigue the ladies of the *salons*, to impress the most subtle specialists in philosophy and science, to win over his Jesuit teachers and liberal Churchmen in general, and to commend his humanitarian project to leaders of state.

To cater for this heterogeneous readership Descartes would somehow fuse into a convincing unity the most heterogeneous materials, manuscripts written for different purposes and at different times over the past eight years. Ironically, this method of composition, which used 'de vieilles murailles...bâties à d'autres fins' (2,1: 15-16), would be quite the opposite of the rational method portrayed in Part 2.

Furthermore, in this process of composition Descartes could not completely be his own master. He wished to avoid metaphysical controversy at this, the first stage of his campaign to reform philosophy and science, but his publisher prevailed upon him to publish his proofs of the existence of God and thus bore much of the responsibility for the inclusion of Part 4 and for the subsequent problem of integrating this sketch of the 'ordre des raisons' into a work intended only to speak about Descartes's ideas. And it was the political and religious climate in France which was the main factor that overcame his reluctance, born of the desire to avoid fruitless controversy (*1*, IV, p.536), to write on ethics. At the last moment the prudent Descartes felt obliged to compose a new part, Part 3, intended to show that his methodical doubt was not a dangerous scepticism subversive of ethics, religion and State. Thus he gave himself the problem of integrating into what was implicitly 'le projet d'une science [= knowledge] universelle qui puisse élever notre nature à son plus haut degré de perfection' (such was the original title of the *Discours* (*1*, I, p.339)) a part concerned with 'une morale imparfaite' adapted to the needs of the uncertain and the *contingent (see below, p.38).

As one can see, the redactional problems Descartes faced were enormous. It was therefore hardly surprising that he was not able to solve all of them completely. In Part 4, for example, he simply could not, as he admitted, satisfy his heterogeneous readership. Here the need to spare the philosophically inept the perils of methodical doubt conflicted with the need to give specialists a brief exposition of a metaphysics which exemplified the 'ordre des raisons', and the result was an obscure account which satisfied neither category.

On other occasions it was the task of rapidly unifying his heterogeneous materials that posed Descartes intractable problems. Three such occasions stand out, the first concerning Part 6. Descartes was not able completely to adapt to the needs of the *Discours* a preface to the *Dioptrique* and the *Météores* written in the winter of 1635-36 when he was thinking of publishing these two essays as a sample of his science. This preface, which became Part 6 of the *Discours*, does not in fact provide a conclusion to the *Discours* and its three essays; thus the *Discours*, which begins boldly and sententiously (if ironically), ends in bathos. Again, Part 6 appears to repeat much of the contents of Part 1 without any acknowledgement that it is doing so and, in the process, renders the very existence of that part, which is in effect a second preface, problematic. Indeed, Part 6, in which Descartes states that his metaphysical speculations and his philosophical ethics are his own affair (6,2: 27-32) appears to rule out the very existence of Parts 3 and 4 (which of course, at the time the preface was written, Descartes had no intention of publishing).

The second occasion concerns Part 1. On one important point Descartes did not revise in the light of his post 1628 experience the 1628 manuscript which provided the substance of Part 1 (beginning, as the 'join' shows, at paragraph 6). The result was a contradiction between the manuscript's condemnation of extensive foreign travel (1,8: 132-33), written when Descartes hoped to settle in Western France, and Descartes's own wanderlust and Dutch 'exile' after 1628.

Finally, a third occasion, which concerns Part 3. Not surprisingly, the late insertion of this part led to certain repetitions and contradictions. The last paragraph of Part 3 being in essence a restatement of the last paragraph of Part 2, Part 4 was now, in effect, introduced twice. And the suggestion in Part 1 that most occupations are vain and useless (1,3: 41-43) could now be contrasted with the refusal in Part 3 to comment on others' occupations (3,5: 122-23), and the hostility in Part 1 to *Stoicism (1,10: 162-70) with the extolling in Part 3 of the moral independence of the ancient Stoics (3,4: 106-19); clearly, between 1628 and 1636 Descartes's attitude to Stoicism had changed.

However, the occasions on which Descartes was not able fully to overcome the problems facing him merely serve to demonstrate their gravity and so to point up his overall achievement in creating out of the most heterogeneous elements no mere mosaic, but a living work which conveys the very soul of his philosophy/science. For Descartes's concern was with 'l'homme concret, engagé, corps et âme, dans l'univers [et] la pensée de Descartes est autre chose que le Cartésianisme; l'intuition qui l'entraîne est plus une exigence à satisfaire qu'un thème ineffable à exprimer, moins une vision du monde qu'un attitude devant le monde' (8, pp.209-10). It was the special genius of the *Discours*, with its unique mixture of the philosophical and the autobiographical, to depict the uniquely non-academic spirit of a philosophy which seeks for truth amongst practical men and which is yet, as is shown for example by the inextricability of the psychological and logical elements of Cartesian method and by the use made of the 'poêle' image (see

16   *Discours de la Méthode*

below, pp.29-30 and 17), intensely personal. We may now ask how Descartes was able, by what I have called his 'art de persuader', to turn an *œuvre de circonstance* into a masterpiece. Hasty judgment — 'précipitation' — and biased judgment — 'prévention' (2,7: 199) — being for Descartes the faults responsible for error, his most general philosophical aim in the *Discours* must be to make his readers aware of these faults and so facilitate their removal. Since it is in childhood that they are consolidated, what better way to insinuate his views than to adopt the mode of autobiography? Descartes's autobiographical presentation of his ideas will therefore be the main weapon in his rhetorical armoury. By describing in Parts 1 and 2 his own progress from childhood to manhood, his rejection of his schooling and the argument from authority, Descartes both prudently attenuated the philosophical points he was making and aroused the curiosity of his readers, especially the non-specialists. These were delighted to discover, in Pascal's phrase, a man rather than an author, a man what is more who had been through the same educational mill as they themselves, and was able to formulate concise criticisms of it which concorded with their own. Descartes's *moi* was thus presented implicitly as both general — representing a whole generation — and universal — representing the progress of a philosophical Everyman. It became the *fil conducteur* of the work, unifying its heterogeneous sources.

What is the nature of this rhetorical weapon, the autobiographical mode? Descartes presents his account of his life as a 'tableau' of 'les chemins que j'ai suivis' (1,4: 56-57), as an 'histoire', related with 'franchise', which is also a 'fable' (1,5: 66-72) in that some of it is to be imitated by the few who can 'suivre un dessein' (6,6: 306) like his. 'Tableau' implies neither strict, that is to say complete, historical truth, nor falsification, but rather stylisation and schematisation. A 'tableau' cannot contain everything, and has to put some things in the foreground and others in the background: in the *clair/obscur* style the former are highlighted and the latter left in the shadows. What the 'tableau' highlights will be, to use a Rabelaisian phrase, the 'substantifique moelle' of his 'histoire', its general and universal import. What the 'tableau' leaves in the shadows will be what contributes nothing to this import or what would deaden its impact. But what is in the shadows, though invisible, is still there; it has not, strictly speaking, been suppressed. As Gouhier stresses (*8*, pp.24-26), Descartes is not baring his soul in an Augustine-like confession, he is not even claiming to write, in the strict sense of the word, an autobiography. He is writing about the past to explain the present, and therefore describes how he became a Cartesian only when this 'how' can also be presented as a 'why', a reason others can acknowledge as of general import. Thus there is no mention of the influence of the Dutch mathematician Beeckman upon his thought (1618), nor of the interview (1627) with Cardinal de Bérulle that encouraged him to promulgate his work (see below, pp.47-48), nor of the three 'poêle' dreams that gave him his sense of intellectual mission (1619). Besides, an anonymous author could not 'name names'.

Schematisation, to be understood here as the subordination of the 'how' — the complexities of 'histoire' — to the 'why' — the overriding intellectual purpose of the work — is anyway inevitable in all accounts of the past, and is inevitably structured by certain *idées reçues* of its times. In Descartes's case, these were the conquering individualism of Machiavelli, which shows itself in the theme of will (e.g. 2,6: 195) seconded by fortune (1,3: 31-32; 2,1: 6; 6,4: 200-01), and the critical individualism of Montaigne (though Descartes gave a new content to Montaigne's introspection and doubt). The latter theme shows itself in the three-stage schema (a) false certainty — school booklearning — leading to 'doutes' and the realisation of his 'ignorance' (1,6: 79-82), followed by (b) experience of 'le grand livre du monde' (1,14: 211), followed by (c) true certainty — knowledge of the *moi* in the methodical doubt of the 'poêle' (2,1: 7). Here the four rules of the Method and the 'maximes' of the 'morale par provision' were, supposedly, established — a rhetorical fiction useful in the case of the Method to symbolise intellectual withdrawal from society's received wisdom and, in the case of both, to situate their rules at a point in time and space.

Providing that the reader accepts Descartes's account of his

character and of the origins of his thought as the work of art it
is, no harm is done. Misunderstandings arise only when readers
take his account as literal truth, believing for example that
Descartes really was — that is to say, was nothing but — the
hero of resolution, circumspection and modesty he portrays
himself as, or, more importantly, that it was scepticism that
played the most important part in the origins of Cartesianism. In
fact, as 1,10: 157-58 and Part 6 indicate, Descartes's thought
moved not so much from doubt to certainty as from certainty to
certainty. Ironically, many readers would appreciate this fact
more if instead of the autobiographical details of the earlier
parts, intended to dramatise the ill effects of *Scholasticism and
the discovery of the Method, they had before them only 6,6
(especially lines 318-25), where there is no talk of Descartes's
schooling leading to scepticism, but rather of the rote learning of
merely probable truths having the fortunate effect of making
Descartes think for himself and thus discover truths that were
certain (cf. *1*, X, pp.372-79).

The decision to adopt the autobiographical mode clearly
determined the style and tone of the work. Descartes would
attempt to recreate the 'unpedantic' — that is to say,
unscholastic — style and tone he had employed and enjoyed in
conversation with learned friends. However, as we have seen,
the *Discours* was meant not only for these but also, and
principally, for a wider audience: for specialists, who did not
always in the early seventeenth-century scientific atmosphere of
rivalry and suspicion behave as scholars and gentlemen, and to
whom Descartes did not always show forbearance and
fairmindedness; and for non-specialists, who often needed to be
led by the hand and reminded gently that the author engaging
them in an *honnête* conversation was their intellectual superior.
And Descartes was, as ever, engagingly or infuriatingly himself,
a fascinating unity of contradictions, both the haughty, ironic
figure of the Frans Hals portrait in the Louvre, and the friendly
honnête homme of the Groeningen Lievens portrait. Yet,
paradoxically, much of the charm of the *Discours* springs from
this impossibility of maintaining a consistent tone of voice —
from the variety of tones adopted according to the needs of the

moment.

For, an *honnête* conversation implies presence, equality and shared interests, often (such is human nature) reinforced by flattery and defined in contradistinction to those of another group. Descartes does all he can to acknowledge the presence of his readers and to incorporate them into the presentation of his ideas. The Introduction sets the tone here by presenting the six parts more as pauses for breath than as chapters. Thereafter, Descartes will be at his reader's side, considerate and caring (e.g. 5,6: 166-67), constantly anticipating his reaction — surprise, criticism or whatever (2,2: 61; 3,6: 170-71; 4,1: 1; 5,4: 117; 6,5: 217; 6,7: 329; 6,10: 421; 6,11: 455) — and skilfully using the Scholastic terms he is familiar with (1,2: 29-30; 4,4: 90-91). Equality is established by professions of modesty (1,4: 50; 2,6: 166; 2,9: 268-69; 6,2: 26-27), by taking the reader into his confidence (6,4: 157-59), and by presenting himself as discreet and peaceful (5,1: 3-9; 6,1: 4).

At the same time, Descartes cannot present himself simply as one *honnête homme* amongst others. He has to appear confident and competent so as to inspire confidence in his enterprise; and this need entails demonstrating his superiority. Thus he stresses the 'satisfaction' (1,3: 44) and 'contentements' (3,5: 128; cf. 2,10: 279) his philosophy has given him, the legitimacy of his hopes for the future (1,3: 44-49), the pressure of friends and correspondents as a reason for publication of his views (3,7: 211-12; 6,8: 375-78). And he makes the boldest claims for his physics (5,1: 22-25; 6,2: 39-56), claims that some readers felt to be boasts. He tells the public quite bluntly that it is their duty to help his enterprise, that virtue is as virtue does (6,3: 144-46; cf. 3,2: 25-33). And his pride shows through all his protestations of modesty; he can be condescending (4,6: 150-55), ironic (1,1: 2-4), polemical (4,7: 167-72), and heated (5,9: 313-62). So much was at stake for the Descartes of 1637 that the urbane tone sometimes slips and aggressiveness, which was as much a part of his character as *bonhomie*, shows through.

Finally, the affirmation of shared interests. Descartes was not above flattering his readers (6,11: 465-68) or exploiting their scorn for Scholastic 'futility' (1,14: 217-26; 2,1: 45-52; 6,6:

281-95). But his main concern was to express the development in ideas from the 'je' of Part 1 — my thoughts — to the 'nous' of Part 6 — our world, of which we could be 'comme maîtres et possesseurs' (6,2: 55-56). And within the parts themselves this movement is cunningly contrived, as in Part 4, where there is a general progression from 'je' (4,1: passim) to 'plusieurs' (4,6: 148) to 'des hommes' and 'les meilleurs esprits' (4,7: 167, 183) to 'nous' (4,8: passim), or in Part 5 where, when dealing with the difference between men and animals, Descartes moves from 'je' to 'nous' in order to appeal to our innate anthropocentrism (5,10: 381-83; 5,11: passim).

Thus the reader has the impression of listening to an individual voice, and the personal tone of the work is reinforced by a skilful mixing of tenses and rhythms and by an effective, because economical, use of imagery. All of these serve to express Descartes's thought clearly or to render it ambiguous or even obscure, according to the needs of the moment. First, the mixing of tenses and rhythms. Here a few general remarks and a few examples must suffice. We may note first that often the past historic is used to subordinate autobiography to the work's philosophical message, to make events represent reasons (e.g. 1,6: 78; 1,14: 208): as one would expect, Part 2, describing the intellectual progress Descartes has made, uses the past historic more than Part 1, which describes what he underwent. The imperfect is used to describe the rules of the Method and the 'maximes' of the 'morale par provision' in order to stress their personal nature; but the future and the present are used to elaborate on the Method's rules because the fruits of the Method belong to everyone. The present tense is often used to stress that his experience is still relevant, or to make intemporal, sententious statements: Part 2 uses the present tense to link 1619 to 1637, historical present to true present, and historical present to intemporal present. And the fact that it is not always possible to distinguish clearly these uses of the present is a fruitful ambiguity that ties the past, the present and the future together and allows the work to speak to the present of its readers in any century. The rhythm of the *Discours*'s sentences also usually has an important persuasive function, as in the account of 'ces

longues chaînes de raisons' (2,8: 215-24), where the long
sentence, with its multiplicity of relative clauses, expresses the
confident link-by-link and linear progress of the Method and so
inspires confidence in the reader. Only occasionally do long
sentences serve to obscure Descartes's thought (1,3: 31-38) or
express his embarrassment (6,1: 1-17).

Finally, the imagery of the *Discours*. Only in one case is this
merely ornamental (2,6: 177-79). Usually, expressing the
subordination, discussed above, of 'histoire' to the overriding
intellectual purpose of the work, it is, as Francc argues, both
emotive and illustrative (*49*, p.64). There are three main images,
those of war, the way, and the house. On the level of 'histoire',
the image of the search for truth as a war in which Descartes is a
general, expresses the most unacademic spirit of an ex-soldier
(e.g. 6,4: 183-95). But this sense is subordinated to the
expression of the conquering nature of his thought; the image of
war rouses the reader to replace war between men with the
manipulation of nature for human needs and delight, and thus,
paradoxically, evokes the peaceful, humanitarian science to
which Descartes has devoted his life (6,12: 479-84).

However, the central images of the work are those of the way
and the house, and these are inseparable. Descartes sees his
'chemin' (e.g. 1,4: 56), 'le droit chemin' of the Method (1,1: 17),
as distinguishing his thought from that of the Scholastics, whose
disputes, as we say, 'get nowhere' (6,5: 236-42). His 'chemin'
leads through the 'ténèbres' (2,5: 155) of the forest (3,3: 59) to
the light of the clearing where his own house is being built (2,2:
77-79; 2,3: 106-08) and where, to use an Augustinian phrase, the
whole City of Man may be built (2,1: 16-31). 'Chemin' is a
powerful image with both religious and moral resonances, it is
both illustrative of the Method, the way to truth, and emotive —
Descartes's 'chemin' or 'voie' (1,1: 12) is the direction, sense or
meaning of his life and echoes the reader's desire for meaning in
his own life. Furthermore, the ambiguity of 'chemin' (1,3:
32-33; 1,15: 246) assists schematisation by tying together
Descartes's wanderings — the physical 'chemins' — and the
development of his thought — 'le droit chemin' of the Method
(1,1: 17) — in such a way as to suggest that the former were

always subordinated to the latter and that Descartes walked
always slowly, carefully (2,5: 156-57) and, of course, resolutely
(e.g. 2,6: 195), along both. And, on the intellectual level, the
ambiguity of 'chemin' ties together the rational Method and the
reasonable 'morale par provision', in which the second
'maxime' counsels *any* straight path in order to avoid
irresolution.

Finally, the house, one of the most powerful images of
mankind. This is an image illustrative of the essence of
Cartesianism and, indeed, of aesthetic Classicism. And it is also
a richly emotive image in Descartes's hands. The house expresses
in the first place Descartes's 'vertical' conception of knowledge
as rational certainty built not on 'la terre mouvante et le sable'
of our unstable sense experience but on 'le roc ou l'argile' (3,6:
173-74) of firm metaphysical foundations (4,1: 4-5). Such
knowledge reflects the method, order and proportion
established by the will and reason of 'un seul architecte' (2,1:
13), it is not the work of natural, and therefore unplanned
growth as is the tree of Aristotelianism, smothered by the ivy of
its commentators (6,6: 272-75). At the same time the house,
because it is inseparable from the larger unit, the City of Man,
expresses Descartes's democratic conception of knowledge as
open to 'n'importe qui' (see below, pp.31-32) and as the fruit of
cooperation (e.g. 6,2: 80-90). And finally, as an emotive image,
the house expresses Descartes's longing for personal 'assurance'
(1,14: 228) and for a new culture, the future City of Man in
which all the 'commodités qui sont dans les villes les plus
fréquentées' of his times (3,7: 231-32), especially those of
prosperous, bourgeois Holland, will be enjoyed in a far greater
measure (6,2: 58-59) by all this City's inhabitants. Thus the
house is a vision on which Descartes may build his hopes as he
tries to transcend the political and religious turmoil of early
seventeenth-century Europe locked in the Thirty Years War, and
it is an image that appeals across the centuries to the reader's
own desire for certainty and for a better life.

2. From Scholastic Probability to Cartesian Certainty: the Method

Method is the intellectual heart of the *Discours* and the true originality of Descartes's thought. But where is the Method in the *Discours*? Descartes's statement that Parts 4 and 5 show that the Method 's'étend à toutes sortes de matières' is unhelpful because to show is not to demonstrate and the character of the two parts is quite different. And his statement that the Method 'consiste plus en pratique qu'en théorie' refers us to the 'Essais de cette Méthode' which modern editions of the *Discours* rarely carry (*1*, I, p.349). Are we left then only with the (apparent) simplicity, or even banality, of the 'principales règles de la méthode' (Introduction) stated summarily (*1*, IX, p.15) in Part 2, and formulated in the light of an abstruse *essai*, the *Géométrie*, absent from our *Discours*?

Fortunately this is not the case. For firstly, in the *Discours*, as elsewhere, Descartes tells us more what his logical theory is not than what it is, by defining the Method in contradistinction to the methods of the Scholastics; we must therefore refer also to Part 1's 'diverses considérations touchant les sciences' (Introduction) and to Part 2's comments on the *syllogism. And secondly, to appreciate the originality of the Method requires us to consider it in contradistinction to a whole culture, an operation that requires reference to other parts of the *Discours*. Finally, we have the 1628 *Regulae* which, used carefully (for Descartes's logical theory developed between 1628 and 1637), can help us to flesh out the compressed account of the Method given in Part 2, and to correct any misleading impression it may convey.

In the last chapter I suggested that Descartes's account of his youth illustrates his theory of the genesis of error, error arising in the form of 'précipitation' and 'prévention' through misuse of the will. Now, since 'true' method is essentially the correct use of the will in the search for truth, Descartes's account may be

seen as depicting Scholastic lack of method, the false belief that
the 'true' method is being followed, and the dire effects of this
lack and of this illusion. It may be seen too as playing down the
discovery of 'true' method in the joy of mathematics in order to
emphasise this criticism of Scholasticism.

Looked at in this way, Part 1's 'diverses considérations
touchant les sciences' appear as a redrawing of the cognitive
map in order to establish new boundary-lines between rational
truth, opinion and faith. Descartes's aim is not at all to take over
the areas of opinion and faith in the name of rational truth; he is
not a *rationalist imperialist, he does not claim that reason is the
only way to truth, that rational truth is the only truth. As a
result of his survey, whole areas of knowledge, or supposed
knowledge, are declared to lie outside — above, alongside, or
beneath — the domain of the reform of purely rational
knowledge that it is the *Discours*'s task to advocate and illustrate
by its depiction of 'true' method. For, in the light of Descartes's
demanding conception of what rational truth is, these areas
appear to him to be based on faculties, or powers, or even
defects of mind and heart, other than 'true' reason — on faith,
on inspiration, on memory, on custom, on authority, or even on
mere prejudice and verbalism. And, as a result of this survey,
the reader already knows, before reading the four rules, that the
Method can only be the unified, orderly expression of the
natural, useful and self-evident light of reason, and that it has,
as it were, an inbuilt ethical demand. Let us look at these points
in more detail.

First, the realm of religious faith. The relationship between
Cartesian reason and the Catholic faith is so close and
complicated that, though Descartes claimed to have excluded
from the *Discours*'s discussion of method the realm of faith (e.g.
3,6: 156-59), each of our ensuing chapters will have to discuss
some aspect of it. At this point we may note only that Descartes,
wishing to replace Aristotle as the Catholic philosopher, was
inevitably hostile to Scholastic theology, which was largely
Aristotelian; that moreover, quite likely under Oratorian
influence as Gadoffre suggests (*6*, p.79), he saw theology only as
a corpus of revealed truths necessary for salvation, and

therefore rejected the speculative nature of Scholastic theology; that he was, of course, anxious to avoid any Galileo-like confrontation with the theologians that might arise from any trespassing on their domain. His concern in Part 1 is therefore surreptitiously to undermine Scholastic theology, thereby opening the way for a new and fruitful relationship between Catholic faith and Cartesian reason, and enthusiastically to endorse faith's claim to be both the certain and the true way to a supernatural end (1,3: 46-47; 1,7: 116; 1:11: 171-79). Indeed, as he had said in the *Regulae*, 'ce qui a été objet de révélation divine est plus certaine que n'importe quelle connaissance [cf. 1,11: 174-75; 3,6: 157-58]: la croyance qu'on lui témoigne...n'est pas un acte de l'esprit, mais de la volonté' (*1*, X, p.370). It is will which responds to the self-evidence that comes from divine grace rather than from natural light. But the very superiority of faith places it outside, and indeed above, the realm of natural reason, and therefore outside and above the Method, which, as reason rightly conducted (1,1: 12-14), seeks a purely human (1,3: 46-47) certainty 'en cette vie' (1,14: 228-29).

Descartes's education at the Jesuit college of La Flèche also claimed to be a certain and true route, but, this time, to a purely natural end. It claimed to provide 'une connaissance claire et assurée de tout ce qui est utile à la vie' but failed, producing instead 'ignorance', 'doutes' and 'erreurs' (1,6: 75-76, 80, 82). It is this global pretention of what was in his eyes a combination of lack of method and of false method posing as true method that Descartes denounces above all, for the various disciplines may severally be justified, some strongly, some lukewarmly, on grounds other than those of rational certainty (1,7: 99-100, 120-23). Thus eloquence and poetry form a realm outside and, since Descartes implies no inferiority, as it were alongside the Method. They are 'des dons de l'esprit, plutôt que des fruits de l'étude' (1,9: 147-48), a sort of natural rather than, as faith is, supernatural inspiration, and are not useless but rather to be esteemed, eloquence for its 'forces' and 'beautés', poetry for its 'délicatesses' and 'douceurs' (1,7: 109-10). However much Descartes's youthful enthusiasm for poetic inspiration (1,9: 146) may have dimmed by 1637, and however much Cartesian reason is blamed for the withering of that inspiration in the seventeenth and eighteenth centuries, one must recognise that it is on methodological grounds alone that eloquence and poetry are excluded from the *Discours* and that Descartes was, as Gadoffre reminds us, 'un des seuls défenseurs de la libre inspiration poétique au dix-septième siècle' (*6*, p.79).

What however of the great legacy of Renaissance Humanism, the study of the Classics — Greek and Latin, and the fables and histories, with their moral lessons, to the knowledge of which these tongues lead? In his judgment of the Classics Descartes's modernism, in a debate which later in the century was to become the *Querelle des Anciens et des Modernes*, is apparent. Whereas religious faith, and poetry and eloquence, provide present, certain inspiration, erudition provides uncertain knowledge of the past. To base a whole culture on texts that can furnish no more than probabilities and exhortations to virtue, and which cultivate memory rather than reason, is to end by spoiling one's judgment of what is true and what is good (1,10: 165-70) and by making oneself incapable of living fruitfully in one's own century (1,8: 136-37). Descartes therefore rejects the claim that the Classics are essential to produce 'une connaissance claire et assurée de tout ce qui est utile à la vie' (1,6: 75-76), and so rejects their claim to constitute a culture of the mind. In this global sense they are useless and, indeed, without the concomitant cultivation of certainty in the Method, such knowledge is prejudicial to the search for rational truth (*1*, X, pp.372-73; cf. 1,8: 133-35). True, as imaginary travel in time (1,7: 104-08) this knowledge may form judgment by, for example, freeing one from the tyranny, the 'prévention', of 'l'exemple et...la coutume' (1,15: 239). But these good results may be obtained in real life by one's travels in space. Thus the *Discours* sees the Classics as no more than a collection of accomplishments with no principle of unity, and these accomplishments themselves as purely optional; the *Recherche de la vérité* was to be truer to the spirit of Descartes's modernism by declaring them redundant.

What of the remaining areas of knowledge, law, medicine, physics and the other sciences? These 'empruntent leurs principes de la philosophie' (1,13: 191-92) and their knowledge-claims stand or fall therefore with those of Scholastic philosophy. Did this philosophy provide the certain way to rational truth? On the contrary, it represented an accumulation over the years (2,1: 8-31) of purely probable and therefore doubtful opinions (1,12: 180-90; 1,7: 116-18), and exemplified the ill effects of both 'prévention' and 'précipitation'. Arrogantly despising simple truths (6,6: 303-05) and practical life (1,14: 220-26), verbalism was its refuge from reality, from moral seriousness (6,6: 281-87). And verbalism characterised its logic, which was in no sense a certain way to truth.

Mostly useless, and sometimes harmful (2,6: 170-79), this logic was based on the syllogism, a mere machine for reasoning without thinking, a plethora of precepts — there were 192 'modes' of the syllogism — weighing down the memory and dispensing the mind from paying attention to what it was doing (*1*, X, p.406). This fatal divorce between form and contents — the former could be valid and the latter false, and vice-versa — ruled out the syllogistic form of reasoning as a way to rational certainty. And Scholasticism could provide no other way, denying as it did that there could be just one road to rational truth, and putting forward a hierarchy of methods appropriate, in its eyes, to the diversity of the sciences, a hierarchy in which mathematics, far from being the key to true method, was regarded as a discipline capable of a purely 'formal' truth. Thus Scholasticism achieved two signal *contresens*; it made thought mechanical and nature animistic (see below, pp.54-55), and it made formal logic the way to truth and declared a true way to truth merely formal. However, the syllogism was not to be entirely rejected, but to be demoted. As an excellent teaching method and way of expounding truths discovered by other means, it forms part of rhetoric (*1*,X, p.406); indeed the very notion of the 'probable' — that which can be supported by reasons — reveals the intrinsic relationship of syllogism and rhetoric.

Finally, for the sake of completeness, we must mention the case of the occult sciences and the very difference cases of the State and of *mœurs*. The rich occult current of Descartes's day — astrology, chiromancy, geomancy, the Kabbalah, alchemy and magic — he roundly declares to be pure imposture (1,13:

204), the various 'sciences' merely 'mauvaises doctrines, superstitieuses [et] fausses' (1,7: 119-22; 1,13: 200-06). Descartes does not even pose the question whether they display lack of method or false method. As verbalism with no grasp of the real they are beneath the Method and the attention of rational men: the mere establishment of Cartesianism will ensure their demise. As for the realms of the State and of *mœurs*, Descartes is careful to point out that they are outside the scope of the Method's rational reform and indeed that their reform is outside the competence of any private citizen. But here we may leave a subject we shall discuss in Chapter 3.

Now that we know, by contradistinction, something of the nature and range of the Method, we may seek to know the latter more directly. Is it, as is often asserted, a 'mathematical' method? How are the famous four rules to be understood and in what way are they original?

The Method was born in Descartes's joy in mathematics. It was the certainty and the self-evidence he found there, the solid 'fondements' of mathematical reasoning (1,10: 157-58, 161), and the fact that what mathematics knows it knows exhaustively (2,9: 268-74), that led the young Descartes to consider almost as false 'tout ce qui n'était que vraisemblable' (1,12: 189-90) and to judge as unknowable by pure reason what could not be known with certainty. Not surprisingly, many readers have concluded from the *Discours*'s account of the discovery of the Method 'in' mathematics that the Method is itself mathematical. And some have gone on to argue that, since it is mathematical, it is not, as Descartes claimed it was, extendable to other domains such as metaphysics, medicine and physics. For Descartes however, the Method is not an expression of mathematics: rather, mathematics exemplifies the Method. But what mathematics are we talking of here, 'ordinary' mathematics or 'true', 'universal' mathematics (*1*, X, pp.373-79)?

The *Discours*'s presentation of the Method does not make clear that there is an essential difference between the two, and plays down the importance of 'universal' mathematics (cf. 5,2: 35,46) in order to highlight the 'poêle''s four rules. The 'ordinary' mathematics of Descartes's time were split up into the 'sciences

particulières' (2,8: 235-36) of arithmetic and geometry — the so-
called pure mathematics — and astronomy, mechanics, optics, ·
hydraulics and the science of harmony — the so-called mixed
mathematics. For Descartes these 'ordinary' mathematics did
not constitute a coherent system of demonstrated truth (2,8:
234-36), being applied to simply utilitarian purposes (1,10:
159-62). They were of no use in physics (2,6: 179-87), geometry
depending too much on the use of the imagination, and algebra,
like the syllogism, being rule-bound and, what is more, tied to
an antiquated system of notation which Descartes was to
improve substantially as an essential precondition for his
mathematical discoveries.

On the other hand, 'true', 'universal' mathematics is the
science of 'proportions en général' (2,8: 241; cf. 1,10: 159, 161)
which was partially discovered by Greek mathematicians like
Pappus and which, as one general theory of proportions, order,
measure and dimension, led to the great discovery, presented in
the *Géométrie*, of co-ordinate geometry and to the revolutionary
notion of the unity of the sciences, one as the mind is one. It is
this 'true' mathematics that exemplifies the basic requirements
of the Method, for 'il n'y a eu que les seuls mathématiciens qui
ont pu trouver quelques démonstrations, c'est-à-dire quelques
raisons certaines et évidentes': and the Method can only be
learnt by training oneself to think mathematically, by
accustoming one's mind thereby to 'se repaître de vérités' (2,8:
228-31, 233-34).

Yet, for all its importance, even 'true' mathematics is not to
be identified with the Method: Descartes is not saying, of
course, that the seeker after rational truth should cultivate only
mathematics (2,8: 215-34), but mathematics and those subjects
which are capable of attaining a certainty equal to that of
mathematics (*1*, X, pp.365-66). In what sense this injunction
should be understood of physics is explained in Chapter 5. Here
we may note that the Method is not in essence mathematical, but
philosophical, and, to the scandal of Leibnitz and of most
professional philosophers since, contains, as well as a purely
logical element, an important psychological element. For this
'méthode pour bien conduire sa raison' (title) requires the

correct application of the whole mind (1,1: 12-18), of memory
and imagination as well as reason (1,2: 19-24). It is a practical
art of increasing the natural light of the mind (*1*, X, p.361), of
training the mind to keep it attentive (*1*, X, p.406). And, since
the diversity of human opinions arises not from the fallibility of
the intellect (1,1: 4-14) but from the misuse of the will, it is a way
of re-educating the will (2,7: 197-202) by the continual, slow
(1,1: 16) overcoming of those factors, 'prévention' and
'précipitation', that can 'offusquer notre lumière naturelle, et
nous rendre moins capables d'entendre raison' (1,15: 240-42).
Flair and knack are essential to use it, for the Method is as
worthless without talent (2,3: 113-29) as talent is useless without
the Method (1,1: 12-14; cf. *1*, X, p.371).

It is because the Method is a practical art with an intrinsic
psychological element that Descartes often appears to be
asserting dogmatically what should, rather, be proved. For
example, seeing what he calls 'natures simples' or 'propositions
simples' (*1*, X, pp. 407-30) — the final goal of the Method's
analysis — as natural to the mind, he does not explain
adequately this fundamental aspect of his logical doctrine. The
Discours merely alludes to these natures (6,3: 105-06; 5,1: 19-20)
and I shall refer to them only to the extent necessary to elucidate
the work. Again, Descartes assumes that the mind knows
naturally what intuition and deduction, the twofold activity of
the mind in the Method (see below, pp.32-33), are and how to use
them, and that, as truth is perceived in the act of intuition, truth
cannot be defined apart from that act. And, a final example, if
one finds 'quelque difficulté' (4,3: 61) in distinguishing an idea
that is clear and distinct and therefore true (see below, p.33)
from one that merely appears to be so and is therefore false, the
only remedy is practice. Those who wish to 'suivre un dessein
semblable au mien' (6,6: 306) must train their minds as he
trained his, applying their minds with order to 'les choses qui se
présentent' (2,1: 51-52; cf. 1,14: 215-16), seeking out practical
men (1,14: 212-13), artisans (*1*, X, pp.403-04), and passing from
mathematics, where self-evidence and certainty are most easily
to be found (2,8: 224-32), to the other sciences (2,10: 279-87).
There is no other, easier way to rational truth, no set of *passe-*

partout rules to be learnt by rote and applied mechanically as, in Descartes's view, the syllogism was applied.

It follows from this, and from the *Discours*'s aim simply to speak about the Method not to teach it, that Descartes's presentation of his rules as 'lois' (2,1: 42; 2,6: 190) always 'fort étroitement observées' (2,6: 192) is to be understood as an aspect of the work's schematisation, a dramatic way of underscoring the need for order and will. It is as a brief description of the essentials of a Method that, in its broad lines, dates back to 1619 and beyond (in its broad lines, because the four rules reflect the 1636 *Géométrie*, Rule 3 applying the principle of the formation of equations and 2,8: 245-57 referring to that *essai*) rather than as a literal 'histoire' of Descartes's practice over the years, that the four rules are invaluable. What is more, the four rules are the key to a Method that expresses a new conception of reason and, since with the Scholastics Descartes sees man as essentially a rational animal (1,1: 5-9; 1,2: 23-30), of man himself — modern (Western) man, as opposed to mediaeval or Renaissance man.

For, as Schouls suggests (*35*, pp.1-9), the four rules announce a new way of thinking which grants a new independence to human reason and aims at mastery over nature, and this new forward-looking way of thinking is far more important than any supposed conflict in the seventeenth century between 'rationalists' and *'empiricists': thus the 'rationalist' Descartes's way of thinking is found, later in the century, in the 'empiricist' Locke. By the radical individualism it displays in Rule 1's criterion of truth — the immediate experience of a thinker free from the sway of majority opinion (2,4: 148-51), intellectual authority (1,14: 207-09) and tradition — in Rule 2's analysis — the reduction of problems to basic, indubitable, individual truths — and in Rule 3's synthesis — the recomposition of knowledge in terms of these truths — the Method corresponds to, and expresses on the *epistemological level, the religious, political and economic individualism of its day.

Of course, Descartes did not claim to have invented the essential procedures of the Method, analysis and synthesis: on the contrary, he saw the antiquity of his principles as pointing to their innateness in reason (*1*, X, pp.375-76). Nor would he understand our preoccupation with originality. Methodical doubt enjoins not universal rejection but universal examination (2,2: 72-77), and what gave Descartes the most satisfaction about his Method was not its novelty but that 'par elle, j'étais assuré d'user en tout de ma raison' (2,10: 280). Nevertheless, he was the first to give striking and influential expression to this new way of thinking and so make it accessible to 'n'importe qui' (*1*, X, pp.371-72; cf. 1,1: 15-18). He was the first to found a whole philosophy upon this new way, and the first to see as inseparable on the one hand the expression of this new way as the key to a new philosophy and a new culture, and, on the other, the refutation of the old way, the old philosophy and the old Classics-based culture. For, if Descartes's criterion of self-evidence is valid, all previous philosophical systems, as uneasy combinations of the certain, the probable and the merely conjectural, are false, and all previous cultures, lacking clear rational guidance, are defective.

If we see the four rules as describing a broad twofold movement of the mind, analysis in Rule 2 and synthesis in Rule 3, rather than as prescribing precise courses of action useful to a user of the Method, we may see the first rule, usually called the rule of self-evidence, as describing the criterion of truth implied in Rules 2 and 3, and the fourth rule, usually called the rule of enumeration, as referring to a process that occurs in Rules 2 and 3 and which should be considered along with intuition and deduction which also occur there. For, as Beck argues (*14*, p.175), Rule 2 uses successive movements of enumeration, deduction and intuition, Rule 3 successive movements of intuition, deduction and enumeration. We may therefore look first at these operations of the mind, and then at the rules of analysis and synthesis.

The *Discours* aiming to avoid technical, latinate vocabulary, there is in the four rules no mention of 'les deux opérations de notre entendement, l'intuition et la déduction' (*1*, X, pp.400-01), that are presupposed and facilitated by the Method. Instead of describing the 'how' — these operations which grasp clear and distinct ideas — the *Discours* points to the 'what' — these ideas themselves. Nevertheless, if we are to understand the Method and its applications in metaphysics and in physics we must be familiar with intuition and deduction, noting that Descartes uses these terms in a new, etymological sense and that the use of two terms does not imply two separate operations of the mind; the two are in essence identical.

Intuition is intellectual vision, 'le concept que l'intelligence pure et attentive forme avec tant de facilité et de distinction qu'il ne reste absolument aucun doute sur ce que nous comprenons...concept qui naît de la seule lumière de la raison' (*1*, X, p.368). When the two conditions for intuition, namely that its objects should be apprehended 'clairement' and 'distinctement' (Rule 1) and that they be apprehended not successively but all at once, are met, the result is self-evidence, 'évidence'. The clarity of an idea is not a mere attribute of that idea, but the immediate presence of that idea in an attentive mind, and the distinct idea is one that is 'tellement précise et différente de toutes les autres qu'elle ne comprend en soi que ce qui paraît manifestement à celui qui la considère comme il faut' (*1*, IX, p.44), that is to say, with attention. One can see now why Descartes writes 'clairement et ...distinctement' (Rule 1); an idea can be clear without being distinct, but the inverse is not possible.

Deduction is the natural movement of thought by which intuition is, as it were, led out, 'un mouvement continu et sans aucune interruption de la pensée qui voit nettement par intuition chaque chose en particulier' (*1*, X, pp.369-70). Thus, though intuition, as intellectual vision, appears to be static, and deduction, as 'toute conclusion nécessaire tirée d'autres choses connues avec certitude' (loc. cit.) appears essentially to be a process, the difference between the two lies in the degree of complexity of the reasoning involved; thus, when intuition grasps a 'proposition simple' like the *cogito* (see below, pp.53-54) there is a certain movement of thought.

As reasonings become more complex, deduction needs, it appears, to be supplemented by enumeration, an operation of which Rule 4 gives a very inadequate idea, presenting it above all as revision; enumeration ensures by 'des revues si générales' that we have left nothing out. For, as our deductions become successively more remote from their starting-point, 'il n'est pas facile de nous rappeler tout le chemin qui nous y a conduits; c'est pourquoi...il faut remédier à la faiblesse de la mémoire par une sorte de mouvement continu de la pensée' (*1*, X, p.387). This movement will aim at a simultaneous vision of the whole deductive series, a vision, then, that will be as much like intuition as possible. Enumeration in this sense therefore differs from deduction in as much as it involves a backwards movement, but appears to be in essence identical with it in as much as it is a 're-visioning' of deductions already made, and has as its main function that of increasing the mind's ability to intuit truth (*1*, X, pp.388-91). However, enumeration has also another role, very important in Descartes's metaphysics and in his scientific method, but to which Rule 4's talk of 'des dénombrements si entiers' merely alludes: that of ensuring that we have left nothing out *before* we begin to solve a problem. It is enumeration in this sense that teaches us 'à suivre le vrai ordre, et à dénombrer exactement toutes les circonstances de ce qu'on cherche' (2,9: 275-77). For it is 'la recherche de tout ce qui se rapporte à une question proposée', the setting-out, both sufficient and methodical, of the conditions upon which the solution of that question depends (*1*, X, pp.388-91).

Finally, Rules 2 and 3, the so-called rules of analysis and synthesis, that together constitute the Method as defined in *Regula 5*, where we read that 'toute la méthode consiste dans l'ordre et l'arrangement des objets sur lesquels il faut faire porter la pénétration de l'intelligence pour découvrir quelque vérité' (*1*, X, pp.379-80). For the Method *is* order (6,6: 311-12), not the Scholastic order of classification but the dynamic order of discovery in which each term depends on the one before it in the 'longues chaînes' (2,8: 215) or networks of reasons, and determines the one that follows. Because the Method observes the 'ordre des raisons', because, as Bréhier says, 'for the real order of production [Descartes] substitutes the order that legitimatises our affirmations concerning things' (*41*, p.61), and because this order is not imposed upon the mind but is nothing but the mind working naturally and fruitfully, the Method is applicable to all the sciences and, in principle, to all rational knowledge.

The rule of analysis contains 'le principal secret' of the Method (*1*, X, pp.381-87). It is by Rule 2 that, 'cherchant premièrement des choses faciles (6,6: 316)...nous ramenons graduellement les propositions compliquées et obscures à des propositions plus simples' (*1*, X, pp.379-80). The rule of analysis describes then a process of reduction, of resolution, of gradual division. For 'toutes les choses peuvent être distribuées en certaines séries...en tant qu'elles peuvent être connues les unes par les autres', and analysis enables us, in each serial order, to 'remarquer ce qui est le plus simple et comment tout le reste en est plus ou moins ou également éloigné' (*1*, X, p.381). Analysis seeks 'les objets les plus simples et les plus aisés à connaître' (Rule 3) which are necessary in order best to solve the problem in question (Rule 2). These objects of thought are 'les plus aisés à connaître' not of course in the sense of being immediately at hand — on the contrary, they are the fruit of the demanding process of analysis — but in the sense that they are prior in the order of deduction and that, as *Regula* 6 explains not altogether satisfactorily (*1*, X, pp.381-87), they are more 'absolute' than those 'relative' notions that depend on them; only 'natures simples' or 'propositions simples' — the final goal of analysis — are intrinsically simple, because knowledge of them does not depend upon the knowledge of anything else.

It is by Rule 3 that, 'partant de l'intuition [des propositions] qui sont les plus simples de toutes, nous tâchons de nous élever par les mêmes degrés à la connaissance de toutes les autres' (*1*, X, pp.379-80), propositions which are 'plus difficiles' (6,6: 317). Rule 3 describes then a process of synthesis, composition or combination, whose task it is to make explicit, to demonstrate what analysis has discovered. To reconstitute the original problem — and, by extension, to reconstruct the whole edifice of rational knowledge — in terms of the clear and distinct elements provided by analysis, we must place the truths acquired in an order which is successively more 'relative' because successively further away from the most 'absolute' notions that began the series, an order that results in the solution of that problem. Usually this order is the natural order of ideas, but sometimes, in problems artfully posed to test our ingenuity (*1*, X, p.435), we must, in order to 'conduire par ordre' (Rule 3) our thoughts, invent an order and not depart from it. For, and this is Descartes's last word on the whole subject of method, 'il vaut mieux ne jamais penser à chercher la vérité d'aucune chose plutôt que de le faire sans méthode' (*1*, X, p.371).

3. Ethics

Whereas the account in Part 2 of the Method presents us with cryptic rules needing much elucidation from other sources, Part 3 gives us quite a full account of what were (the Introduction is misleading here) the principal maxims of Descartes's 'morale par provision' (*1*, IX, p.15; 3, 1: 10-11). However, to understand these maxims it is not sufficient to analyse them in themselves. Rather, one must decide how they fit into what one might call the dynamic moral context of the *Discours*.

As a brief consideration of the various senses in which these maxims are provisional shows, they may be seen as the first stage in the elaboration of a philosophy which is, true to the etymological sense of the word, 'l'étude de la sagesse' (*1*, IX, p.2). In the first place, the three maxims are provisional in that they are necessary while Descartes is eradicating 'toutes les opinions que j'avais reçues jusques alors en ma créance...afin d'y en remettre par après, ou d'autres meilleures, ou bien les mêmes, lorsque je les aurais ajustées au niveau de la raison' (2,2: 72-77); for 'par provision' means, Richelet's *Dictionnaire* of 1680 tells us, 'fourniture de choses nécessaires pour quoi que ce soit'.

Secondly, as the 'conclusion' (3,5: 120) to the 'morale par provision' makes clear, the three maxims are provisional in that Descartes is all the time resolutely looking for better ones; for, as we know, the Method has an inbuilt moral demand.

Thirdly, both the three maxims and their 'conclusion' are provisional in the sense that all Descartes's pre-1629 science was provisional; they precede the attainment of metaphysical certainty. Metaphysics will make important contributions to Cartesian ethics but, more fundamentally, will make possible the elaboration of a new philosophy/wisdom of which the *Discours* gives a foretaste. For it is implicitly, as we have seen, 'le Projet d'une science universelle qui puisse élever notre nature à son plus haut degré de perfection' (*1*, I, p.339), and the expression of a desire to serve humanity by placing physics, mechanics and medicine on firm, rational foundations. As the preface to the 1647 *Principes de la philosophie* tells us, by philosophy/wisdom 'on n'entend pas seulement la prudence dans les affaires, mais une parfaite connaissance de toutes les choses que l'homme peut savoir, tant pour la conduite de sa vie, que pour la conservation de sa santé et l'invention de tous les arts' (*1*, IX, p.2).

And finally, for the sake of completeness, we may note that, after the attainment of metaphysical certainty, Descartes's ethics will be at any point provisional in that it is developing with Cartesianism as a whole and is not yet the ideal, 'definitive' ethic which, Descartes hoped, would one day crown his philosophical edifice (*1*, IX, p.14) but which steadily receded from sight as he came up against the ever-increasing difficulty of extending his scientific knowledge (e.g. 6,3: 136-41).

At first sight then, there is between the 'morale par provision' and later moral reflection perfect continuity, a process of slow improvement from that 1619 ethic, 'une morale imparfaite, qu'on peut suivre par provision pendant qu'on n'en sait point encore de meilleure' (*1*, IX, p.15), to the posited ideal ethic. This process is marked by a qualitative jump when in 1629 the metaphysics, grounding truth and goodness in the divine nature, makes possible a transposition of the three maxims, which accepted 'les opinions les plus modérées' of others (3,2: 16-17) and the need to follow one's own 'opinions les plus douteuses' (3,3: 56) to, in the 1640s, a new major key of rational moral autonomy in which virtue is to do all the things one judges to be the best.

However, this process is not as unproblematic as it seems. The post 1637 fate of the 'morale par provision', in which a provisional ethic is, somehow, transposed into a rational one, is outside our remit. But the origins of the 'morale par provision', and the relationship of the post 1629 ethic to the sciences within Descartes's philosophy/wisdom, are not, and merit scrutiny. Our first question must therefore be, how satisfactory is Descartes's justification of the 'need' for 'une morale par provision'? How could Descartes, as the Introduction claims, have 'tirée' his three maxims from the Method as described in Part 2? What connection can there be between two sets of rules which are apparently quite different in nature? For, on the one hand, there are four rules outlining the individual's independent path to rational truth, condemning 'la précipitation et la prévention' (2,7: 199) and orientated, what is more, towards the needs of the *Géométrie*. And, on the other, there are three maxims of an ethic designed to make moral resolution and happiness possible while resolute judgment is impossible and so advocating (Maxim 2) action that looks very much like 'précipitation', an ethic moreover that is prepared to accept (Maxim 1) others' opinions in the place of one's own and which is — and this looks very much like 'prévention' — never doubted (3,6: 156-59).

Whatever this connection is, it is clearly not the logical one of deduction, for were the three maxims deduced from the Method they would partake of the latter's certainty. 'Tirée' must then mean something less rigorous than 'deduced', and the obvious candidate is the logically ambiguous 'drawn'. In the loosest sense of the word, the three maxims are drawn from the Method in that, quite clearly, the Method is their *raison d'être*, their, to use Aristotelian terms, necessary but not necessarily sufficient cause. The Method requires, in order to overcome 'prévention', 'hardi' (2,3: 113) methodical doubt which participates in the Method's moral purpose (and therefore, Descartes holds, has nothing in common with the 'futile' doubt of the sceptics which is simply *mauvaise foi* (3,6: 170-72)), but which nevertheless would have led to a situation in which resolute action and happiness were impossible (the most important of the 'diverses difficultés' referred to in 2,2: 82) but for the formulation of the 'morale par provision'. In a word, but for the Method, there would be no methodical doubt, and but for methodical doubt, there would be no 'morale par provision'.

In a 'tighter' sense of the word, the maxims are 'drawn' from the Method in that they formulate its intrinsic moral demands of resolution (Maxim 2) — and therefore freedom, see below, p.45 — and joy (Maxim 3) in a situation in which only a lower degree of freedom, resolution and joy is obtainable. Here resolution is not 'précipitation' because, as its introduction (3,1) says, the 'morale par provision' is concerned with resolution in *action* (3,3: 54-55) and presupposes a mind searching the while for better maxims (3,5: 135-37) — a point essential to understand Maxim 1's treatment of religion. When Descartes is obliged by methodical doubt to act as if 'la vraie religion' (2,1: 38) were simply a human institution, this 'as if' operates purely on the level of action, for his faith was never threatened by this doubt (3,6: 157-58). Finally, the three maxims are not 'prévention' because of their intimate link — the two senses of 'drawn' we have discussed — with a Method whose intellectual/moral aim is to overcome 'prévention'.

However, we must now ask whether the Method is in fact a sufficient cause of the 'morale par provision'. And if '*une* morale par provision' (3,1: 10-11) is necessary in order to ensure resolution and happiness, does it have to be this particular one?

Reflecting on these questions, one sees that the 'morale par provision' is more than the ethic of a philosophical Everyman seeking a certain type of rational truth. This ethic is also, and must be, that of a particular man who, having made an act of what one might call philosophical faith, faith in his philosophy, seeks this rational truth inside a particular political and moral/religious framework, both intellectual and institutional. Any philosophy rests on a presupposition, or presuppositions, that cannot be proved by that philosophy itself and is in that sense pre-philosophical. Descartes, at the stage of methodical doubt described in Part 2, does not yet know that the Method will yield the 'fruits' (1,3: 38) it eventually did and enable him to 'conduire ma vie beaucoup mieux' (2,2: 78) — as it did (6,2: 30-31). His philosophical faith, like his religious faith, is in the first instance an act of will, and one which is never doubted and cannot be doubted because it is only this faith that makes doubt, and indeed the elaboration of the whole Cartesian system of natural knowledge, possible. And this act of will to seek certainty in both speculation and conduct (1,14: 226-29) is indissociable from the hope, inspired by early joy in mathematics (1,10: 157-58), that such certainty can be found, and is, because it is being carried out within a moral/religious framework, a moral act.

For Descartes's philosophical faith, his decision to 'conduire ma vie beaucoup mieux', presupposes at least four things: that there is an essential moral nature of man that can be brought 'à son plus haut degré de perfection' (see above, pp.37-38); that this nature is God-given; that the perfecting of this nature by the use of right reason — the Method — is a Christian duty and a Christian joy. And his decision presupposes too of course that there is a realm of private actions separate from the public domain of 'mœurs', the private citizen having the right to 'réformer' the former but not the latter (2,2: 67-77; cf. 6,2: 32-37), at least, not directly (see below, p.43). Let us now look more closely at the moral/religious presuppositions of Descartes's philosophical faith.

Descartes gives two apparently quite different reasons for the three maxims, one practical and one purely moral. The claim that, 'les actions de la vie ne souffrant souvent aucun délai' (3,3: 67-68), this ethic was necessary 'afin que je ne demeurasse point irrésolu en mes actions' (3,1: 7-8) appears to be a purely practical reason. But firstly, a practical need has to be perceived and responded to, and this response requires will, the will that moral action, which is a demand of man's essential moral nature, should not be made impossible by methodical doubt. The first thing that any truthseeker must do is to 'tâcher de se former une morale qui puisse suffire pour régler les actions de la vie, à cause que cela ne souffre point de délai, et que nous devons surtout tâcher de bien vivre' (*1*, IX, p.13). And secondly, irresolution is for Descartes a negative 'passion' (defined by Richelet as an 'agitation...causée dans l'âme par le mouvement du sang et des esprits [see below, pp.73-74] à l'occasion de quelque raisonnement'), a form of fear that destroys contentment. Thus this practical reason presupposes moral reasons.

The second reason given for the ethic, namely that 'je ne laissasse pas de vivre dès lors le plus heureusement que je pourrais' (3,1: 9-10), is indissociable from the first reason and is really both a moral and a religious reason. For Maxims 2 and 3, resolutely observed, will lead to happiness (3,4: 89-91; cf. 3,5:

144-48, 155) and peace of conscience (3,3: 76-81) by freeing him from avoidable occasions for repentance, remorse and regret (3,4: 93-99).

And finally, the 'conclusion' to the 'morale par provision' makes quite clear its moral/religious context: 'Dieu nous ayant donné à chacun quelque lumière pour discerner le vrai d'avec le faux' (3,5: 137-38), that is to say 'la puissance de bien juger' (1,1: 6), it is Descartes's Christian duty and joy to ensure, by the cultivation of the Method, that the 'semences de vérités' (6,3: 105) planted in us by Providence do not fall on stony ground.

It is because the 'morale par provision' is both the ethic of a truthseeker — any truthseeker — and of a particular man who has made certain political, moral and religious options that the three maxims are so heterogeneous. This fact is not, as some critics have thought, to be explained by the assumption that this ethic is a mere expedient, a combination of conformism (Maxim 1) and moderate Stoicism (Maxim 3) hastily patched together to satisfy Church and State. Descartes's prudence (see above, pp.13-14) did not lead him to concoct an ethic, but to stress aspects of an ethic that was already his, for example his political and religious loyalty (Maxim 1) and the need for resolution in action (Maxim 2). Be that as it may, Maxim 1, often called the rule of conformism, is more like a 'maxime' ('sorte d'axiome, sorte de sentence généralement reçue', says Richelet) and has little internal unity, a profession of religious and political conformism being followed by a sensible preference for moderate opinions-in-action, itself followed by a somewhat idiosyncratic expression of dislike for irrevocable personal commitments. However, Maxim 2, often called the rule of resolution, and Maxim 3, often called the rule of autonomy or of happiness, which deal with the more private world of actions ruled by will, are much more like 'règles' ('précepte général sur quoi roule quelque art', says Richelet) — as one would expect from maxims that express the moral *desiderata* of the Method. Furthermore, resolution leading to happiness (3,3: 76-81; 3,4: 82-91), these two maxims are inseparable.

So much then for the origins of the three maxims adopted 'par provision'. But these maxims are also (see above, p.37) provisional in a second sense, namely in that Descartes is the while resolutely looking for better ones — resolution that expresses the inbuilt moral demand of the Method: their function is to help Descartes find more truth and so increase both his knowledge and his joy.

It is of course the status of these maxims that is provisional, not necessarily all their contents (3,5: 141-44). And indeed there is much in these maxims that is always true. For example, it is always the case that the realms of faith, the State and 'mœurs' lies outside the scope of the Method's rational reform and provide the context within which the Method is exercised (Maxim 1). In the political domain and in that of 'mœurs','l'exemple et...la coutume' (1,15: 239), so harmful in the realm of pure reason, have rightful sway, and the most that we, as private citizens, can do, is to 'examiner...toutes les mœurs des lieux où nous vivons, pour savoir jusques où elles doivent être suivies' (*1*, IV, p.295). Politics can never be more than reasonable — born of compromise (2,2: 87-92) — rather than rational — born of the intrinsic order of reason, that is to say of the Method. It is revealing that Descartes writes that 'c'est le plus grand bien qui puisse être en un état, que d'avoir de vrais philosophes' (*1*, IX, p.3) — *in* a state, not directing it, as Plato wished, or proposing rational reforms and advising rulers as the eighteenth-century *philosophes* did. The most that any private citizen can do to change public institutions is to attempt to win over the relevant authorities — in the case of 'l'ordre établi dans les écoles' (2,2: 71-72), the Jesuits.

Again, it is always the case (Maxim 2) that 'les actions de la vie ne souffrant aucun délai..., lorsqu'il n'est pas en notre pouvoir de discerner les plus vraies opinions, nous devons suivre les plus probables' (3,3: 67-70) and that, faced with several equally probable reasons, we must choose one and follow it resolutely (*1*, IX, p.26). And, a final example, it is a truism (Maxim 3) that only our 'pensées', which we may define provisionally as all the operations of the soul, are directly, immediately, within our power.

However, it was only, Descartes stresses, because he was resolutely looking for better rules that he could in good conscience follow his three maxims at all; it was only because he was sure that the Method, leading to 'toutes les connaissances dont je serais capable' (3,5: 146-47; cf. 1,3: 34-38; 2,10: 279-81), would lead also to 'tous les vrais biens qui seraient jamais en mon pouvoir' (3,5: 148) that he was able to bring himself in Maxim 1 to 'me…contenter des opinions d'autrui', in Maxim 2 to follow doubtful opinions, and in Maxim 3 to train himself to 'borner mes désirs [et] être content' (3,5: 135-48).

The immediate and dynamic moral content of the three maxims is thus that of a moral agent who had always had 'un extrême désir d'apprendre à distinguer le vrai d'avec le faux, pour voir clair en mes actions, et marcher avec assurance en cette vie' (1,14: 226-29). Because he was seeking 'une connaissance claire et assurée de tout ce qui est utile à la vie' (1,6: 75-76) he was critical of his education and, by extension, contemporary culture, on account of its lack of any certain moral guidance (2,1: 52-60) and its obscuring of the natural light of reason (1,10: 165-70). Good will was inherent in his 'ferme et constante résolution' (2,6: 195) to observe the rules of a Method which, by augmenting the powers of the mind in both speculation and moral action, gave man what 'en cette vie' (1,14: 228-29) is his highest good, the contemplation of truth and its attendant 'satisfaction' (1,3: 44; 3,5: 133) or 'félicité' (*I*, X, p.361; cf. 3,5: 128-35). As the fourth *Méditation* says, 'si je connaissais toujours clairement ce qui est vrai et ce qui est bon, je ne serais jamais en peine de délibérer quel jugement et quel choix je devrais faire' (*I*, IX, p.46). Or, as 3,5: 151 puts it, in principle 'il suffit de bien juger pour bien faire'.

However, if even in purely intellectual matters there is sometimes 'quelque difficulté' (4,3: 61) in recognising ideas that are truly clear and distinct, the difficulty is far greater in the realm of moral action. Here, if only because it is always the case that 'les actions de la vie ne souffr[ent] souvent aucun délai' (3,3: 67-68) and that our actions are directed towards other beings equally endowed with free will and its consequent unpredictability, we often have to act, and have the duty to act, without being sure that we are in a position to 'bien juger' in 3,5's rigorous sense of the phrase. In practice therefore one must often content oneself with 'juger le mieux qu'on puisse pour faire...tout son mieux' (3,5: 152-53), and strive to 'se fortifier l'entendement pour discerner ce qui est le meilleur en toutes les actions de la vie' (*1*, IV, p.291).

Now for the third sense (see above, pp.37-38) in which the maxims of the 'morale par provision' are provisional. Both the three maxims and their 'conclusion' are provisional in the sense that they precede the attainment of metaphysical certainty which itself contributes to ethics and which makes possible the elaboration of the Cartesian system in which ethics will be the highest branch of the Tree of Knowledge.

It is in metaphysical enquiry that, since 'la volonté et la liberté ne sont qu'une même chose' (*1*, IX, p.148), the thinker, seizing in the *cogito* his existence as both thought and will, *ipso facto* seizes this existence as liberty; that the clear distinction of 'pensée' and 'étendue' gives him certain knowledge of what depends on him as opposed to the working knowledge presupposed by Maxim 3 (the physics will elucidate the interaction of mind and body); that he meets the ultimate foundation of ethics, the God who is reality, truth and goodness, and that he acquires the conditional certainty of the immortality of the soul which religious faith makes an absolute certainty, thus giving ethics a supernatural sanction. Thus the largely implicit moral/religious presuppositions that made his philosophical quest possible have been ratified by reason and may now, as they in fact did in the 1640s, enter explicitly into the elaboration of any future ethic. But more importantly, as far as both the *Discours* and the wisdom it outlines are concerned, metaphysics provides firm rational 'fondements' (4,1: 4-5) for a physics, a mechanics and above all, a medicine that will serve humanity and which have important moral implications. How, we may now ask, is Descartes's post 1629 ethic related to these sciences within the dynamic moral context of the *Discours*? Is medicine, as 6,2 appears to suggest, the 'real' ethic of the *Discours*? Or, as some critics have thought, does 6,2 point to an ethic of human domination over nature that we would now call an ethic of 'scientific humanism'?

Here we must attempt to keep the total moral context of the

Discours in view. Certainly, it is true that for man, 'dont la principale partie est l'esprit' (*1*, IX, p.4), the highest good in this life is the contemplation of truth; that by 'un long exercice et...une méditation souvent réitérée' (3,4: 104-05) the truth-seeker can control his 'passions' and thus the body; that the *Discours* speaks of a method 'pour bien conduire sa raison' in both speculation and action, and that ethics is the highest branch of the Tree of Knowledge. But it is also the case that man's reason is an embodied reason and that the body is both good in itself and the foundation of what the Greek philosophers called the Good Life; that metaphysical and ethical truths can be grasped by very few (*1*, II, p.145) and that very few are capable of the 'long exercice' of 3,4; that philosophical ethics belong to the private domain (6,2: 30-32), enabling one to 'conduire [sa] vie beaucoup mieux' (2,2: 78); that the Method exists principally to 'chercher la vérité dans les sciences', and so in the public domain, that of the State and of humanity in general, and that the *Discours*'s main aim is to further this science in order to benefit all men, present and to come, however undeserving and unintelligent they may be; and that this aim is that of a Christian for whom the cultivation of Method is a God-given duty and joy and who desires to serve humanity in a way appropriate to a philosopher/scientist. Let us look at these points in more detail.

Because man is, in Pascal's phrase, 'ni ange, ni bête, mais homme', a 'substantial union' of two interacting 'substances', mind and body (see below, pp.75-76), in which 'l'esprit dépend si fort du tempérament, et de la disposition des organes du corps' (6,2: 62-63), it is medicine that is the most important science — as the place given in Part 5 to the circulation of the blood indicates. What are the nature and the moral implications of the medicine 'fondée en démonstrations infaillibles' (*1*, I, p.106; cf. 6,2: 76-79) that was 'de tout temps le but principal de mes études' (*1*, IV, p.329)? In the first place, it is no panacea. Though after the stage of the 'morale par provision' there is no longer cause to accept illness as bad 'fortune' (3,4: 83, 99-103), the metaphysics reminds us that 'le doute, l'inconstance, la tristesse et choses semblables' (4,4: 106-07) are inevitable human imperfections. Medicine therefore offers the best hope of moral and intellectual improvement to the generality of men. It may be able to prevent or cure illness and senility, which make the practice of virtue difficult, or, by destroying free judgment, even impossible (6,2: 62-66). And in the second place, Descartes is envisaging not 'medical engineering' by drugs or other means, but natural remedies for the 'conservation' of health, or its 'rétablissement' if lost (*13*, I, p.165; cf. 6,2: 59-62).

An improved medicine then, if it is not the 'real' ethic of the *Discours*, is the most important of the 'connaissances...fort utiles à la vie' promised by the 'philosophie...pratique' that Descartes was seeking in order to make us 'comme maîtres et possesseurs de la Nature' (6,2: 47-56). The same philosophy/wisdom promises us a physics that will harness natural processes to our needs and a mechanics whose 'infinité d'artifices...feraient qu'on jouirait, sans aucune peine, des fruits de la terre et de toutes les commodités qui s'y trouvent' (6,2: 57-59); for the enjoyment of life depends upon adequate leisure, then a luxury enjoyed by the few. What is the nature and scope of what is often called Descartes's 'technological optimism'? Does it point, as some critics have claimed, to a this-worldly ethic of will-to-power over nature, of scientific humanism?

There is no doubt that Part 6 gives the first statement in French (Descartes followed Bacon here) of modern Western man's growing commitment to the mastery of nature, and that this commitment is an important aspect of the new forward-looking way of thinking represented by the Method. Thus, in retrospect, both Parts 2 and 6 may be seen to announce a new direction for Western thought and culture. But Descartes's visionary promises and claims in Part 6 must be seen within their own framework, that of a Christian humanism. Not to have divulged his physics, the 'trunk' of his Tree of Knowledge (*1*, IX, p.14), would have been to 'pécher grandement contre la loi qui nous oblige à procurer, autant qu'il est en nous, le bien général de tous les hommes' (6,2: 45-46) — a phrase that recalls Descartes's Paris interview with Cardinal Bérulle, who strengthened Descartes's conviction that to promulgate his science, which promised so much that was useful to man, was 'une obligation de conscience' (*13*, I, p.165). For it is 'ceux qui désirent en général le bien des hommes' and those alone who are really virtuous (6,3: 144-45), and 'c'est proprement ne valoir rien que de n'être utile à personne' (6,4: 170-71). That is to say, virtue, true 'générosité', is a question of one's deeds not of one's words, of never lacking the will to 'entreprendre et exécuter toutes les choses [qu'on] jugera être les meilleures' (*1*, XI, p.446). The virtue of a philosopher/scientist lies in his vocation to serve mankind by his philosophy/science, and this means principally through his physics, his mechanics and his medicine — principally but not entirely, for, to give but two examples, one reason for the inclusion of the 'morale par provision' in the *Discours* was 'le zèle que j'ai toujours eu pour tâcher de rendre service au public' (*1*, IX, p.15), and Descartes's philosophy has an important apologetic role. And this vocation, rather than prudence or the impossibility of formulating some 'definitive' ethic, was I suspect the basic reason why Descartes is one of the few major philosophers not to have composed a treatise on ethics.

4. Metaphysics

Part 4 is a sketch of the 'ordre des raisons' and the most unsatisfactory part of the *Discours* (see above, p.14). Therefore this chapter is the longest in the book and, following Descartes's advice (*2*, p.13), aims to elucidate his arguments by recourse to the 1647 *Méditations métaphysiques* and indeed to several of his works published after 1637. Part 4 contains what Descartes called the 'fondements' (4, 1: 4-5; cf. Introduction; 3,7: 206-07) of his metaphysics, 'fondements' described loosely in the Introduction as proofs of 'l'existence de Dieu et de l'âme humaine'. However, a 1636 letter is more exact when it describes these 'fondements' as an attempt to 'démontrer l'existence de Dieu et de l'âme séparée du corps' (*1*, I, p.339), for this description points to the vital importance of Descartes's original and rigorous way of distinguishing soul from body — the so-called Cartesian *dualism (see below, pp.54-55).

What is the role of these metaphysical 'fondements' in the *Discours*? 2, 10: 289-93 gives the impression that they exist simply to provide indubitable principles for the sciences. However, as we have seen, the function of the work was both to prepare the way for Descartes's complete Physics and to be one battle in a long campaign to rebuild the House of Knowledge; and the Tree of Knowledge had metaphysical roots. Indeed, the *Discours* shows how Descartes stood out as a scientist in his generation: he would not abandon the traditional view that 'philosophy' covered the whole of natural knowledge. Whereas Galileo's science had, as Descartes complained, no explicit metaphysical foundations and Pascal was shortly to denounce the resort to *a priori* principles in physics, Descartes refused to sever metaphysics and physics but, instead, inverted the relationship that obtained in Scholasticism between physics and metaphysics by basing the former on the latter, and did this by applying one method to 'toutes sortes de matières' (see above, p.23), including metaphysics.

The originality of this metaphysics lies even more in its method than in its conclusions, Descartes proving the superiority of his Method, in part, by its ability to adapt traditional and heterogeneous proofs of God to its own unifying purpose. This originality lies essentially in the fact that the metaphysics exhibits the 'ordre des raisons', that is to say the 'explicit' order of discovery, or knowledge, and not the 'implicit' order of being, in which God, not the *cogito*, comes first (*2*, p.13). Let us then consider briefly Part 4's metaphysics as a sketch of the order of discovery.

Metaphysics begins when doubt, present in the Method as the thinker's ability at any time to withold his assent to what is obscure (Rule 1), is intensified and universalised in the form of a preliminary enumeration (Rule 4) of all the types of knowledge in which doubt is possible. Analysis (Rule 2) discovers the particular truth, the 'nature simple'or 'proposition simple' 'cogito ergo sum' (I think therefore I am), the most simple truth and the easiest to know for one conducting his thoughts 'par ordre' (2,7: 206; 6,6: 311-14). Synthesis (Rule 3) now makes explicit what analysis has discovered and reconstructs the whole edifice of knowledge. From the minimal certainty that one's self-consciousness involves one's existence one moves to the question 'What am I?' and then to the search for an idea that has a necessary cause outside itself — the idea of God — and that will permit one to argue from the essence of things to their existence. For, 'selon les lois de la vraie logique, on ne doit jamais demander d'aucune chose, si elle est, qu'on ne sache premièrement ce qu'elle est' (*1*, IX, pp.85-86), and not vice-versa as the Scholastics thought. Metaphysical reconstruction must move forward from certainty to certainty, from clear and distinct idea to clear and distinct idea, in a logic that is not one of mere words like the sterile formal logic of the Scholastics but a dynamic, generative logic of ideas in which order consists in the fact that 'les choses qui sont proposées les premières doivent être connues sans l'aide des suivantes, et que les suivantes doivent après être disposées de telle façon, qu'elles soient démontrées par les seules choses qui les précèdent' (*1*, IX, p.121). We may now examine in detail the stages in Descartes's metaphysical reconstruction, of which the first is doubt. What is the nature of metaphysical doubt? How does it differ from that of the sceptics? What is its purpose? And what is its scope in Part 4?

In metaphysical doubt, 'l'esprit, usant de sa propre libcrté, suppose que toutes les choses ne sont point, de l'existence desquelles il a le moindre doute' (*1*, IX, p.9). This is not doubt of our ideas — 'natures simples' like 'pensée' or 'existence', or general principles, common notions, like 'pour penser il faut être' (*1*, IX, p.29) or the principle of causality. These are known without proof, simply enregistered by the understanding: they do not provide knowledge of any thing existing outside our thought. Metaphysical doubt is doubt of our judgments, acts of will in which alone, in the strict sense, error and truth are to be found. However, since such doubt is an act of (free) will (4,1: 16, 25), is it not therefore really refusal or even negation, and therefore not doubt at all, let alone sceptical doubt?

Certainly, Descartes's doubt is, as he claims (3,6: 170-74), quite different in essence to the doubt of the sceptics, but — a fact he prudently plays down in the *Discours* (4,1: 30-33) — it uses their reasons for its own purposes. Sceptical doubt is a suspension of judgment practised moderately over a lifetime and is 'complete' in that it doubts both judgments and ideas. For Descartes, doubt must be practised once in one's life (2,2: 74), methodically, and therefore provisionally, in order to draw out the seeds of certainty Providence has planted in our minds (see above, p.42). Seeing no middle ground — probability — between certainty and absence of certainty, Descartes's mind must exhaust all possible reasons for doubt, including those of the sceptics; his doubt is therefore not moderate or reasonable but hyperbolic.

Thus Descartes doubts 'toutes les choses où nous trouverons le moindre soupçon d'incertitude' — and this is 'genuine', unforced doubt. But he will also reject as false 'toutes celles où nous pourrons imaginer le moindre doute' (*1*, IX, p.25; cf. 4,1: 28-29), and this is doubt feigned (4,1: 25) in order to reach absolute certainty. Doubt is a test, a tool that, applying enumeration — the sufficient and methodical setting-out of the conditions upon which the solution of a problem depends (see above, pp.33-34) — lists the realms of knowledge in which doubt may arise and, like an acid, bites into the principles upon which these rest in order to test them all: it is in this sense that metaphysical doubt is 'complete', not in the sense that Descartes regards our faculties as entirely unreliable, or that he attempts the impossible task of considering as doubtful each and every judgment he has ever made, or, of course, that he doubts both ideas and judgments. His doubt is a thwarting of our untutored tendency, through 'précipitation' and 'prévention', to make prejudiced judgments. It is bending a curved stick backwards in order to straighten it, and is therefore negation of all our prejudices — misdirected acts of will, erroneous judgments — and, he claimed, only of our prejudices. Thus it is true that in metaphysical doubt the will refuses, or resists, until it can, before the 'entièrement indubitable' *cogito* (4,1: 14-15), refuse or resist no longer. At least, metaphysical doubt *per se* is like this. But what is the scope of doubt in Part 4? Does it include doubt of the reality of the external world?

Even if we cannot be sure what the scope of Descartes's metaphysical doubt was in 1637, we know that he was unwilling to develop all the reasons for it in Part 4 (see above, pp.13-14). In my view he does hint here at doubt of the reality of the external world, but his deliberately obscure account of his doubt precludes any certainty on this point. Thus, in 4,1's enumeration, three realms are scrutinised, the senses, the intellect and the waking state, but only the last appears to offer serious grounds for doubt. Lines 15 to 17 appear to doubt merely that things are as the senses present them to us — appear, because in 4,8: 224-31 the same doubt leads up to what I take to be a sketch of a proof of the existence of the external world. And the second doubt (4,1: 17-22) appears merely to raise a practical difficulty regarding rational certainty that Descartes himself could but see as derisory (2,9: 271-74). The third doubt (4,1: 22-27; 4,2: 36-38) does appear at least, by putting into question the most common criterion of reality, that of consistency, to involve doubt of the external world. This doubt, based on the possibility of confusing wakefulness and dreaming, is taken up

again in 4,4: 110-11, in 4,7: 178-83 (where the existence of a
veracious God is immediately put forward to refute it), and
again in 4,8: 206-21. However, this doubt can be seen also as
intensifying the second doubt in order to make Descartes's main
point that only 'évidence' is true whether we are awake or
dreaming (4,8: 221-23). Finally, 4,6 and 4,7, in defiance of the
'ordre des raisons', supplement 4,1's inadequate enumeration
after Descartes has proved the existence of God and the real
distinction of soul and body. In fact, 4,6's attack on men's
infatuation with imagination and the senses, and 4,7's rhetorical
challenge to 'les meilleurs esprits' (line 183) to overcome doubt
in any way different to Descartes's own, replace the radical
reasons for doubt given in the *Méditations*.

Doubt having shown, however inadequately in Part 4, that
'[il] nous délivre de toutes sortes de [= all] préjugés, et nous
prépare un chemin très facile pour accoutumer notre esprit à se
détacher des sens, et enfin...qu'il fait qu'il n'est pas possible que
nous puissions plus avoir aucun doute, de ce que nous
découvrirons après être véritable' (*1*, IX, p.9), the scene is now
set for the discovery of 'quelque chose en ma créance, qui fût
entièrement indubitable' (4,1: 14-15). This truth, 'je pense, donc
je suis' (4,1: 31) is discovered in the very act of doubting (4,2:
40-41). Thus 'I doubt therefore I am' is the same as 'I think
therefore I am', Descartes understanding by 'pensée' all
operations of the will, intellect, imagination and senses, 'tout ce
qui est tellement en nous, que nous en sommes immédiatement
connaissants' (*1*, IX, p.124), that is to say one's subjective
experience, and making 'thought' and 'consciousness'
equivalent terms. It is then 'pendant que je voulais...penser que
tout était faux [que] je pris garde [que] moi, qui le pensais, fusse
quelque chose' (4,1: 28-30). The *cogito* cannot be understood
outside the immediate context of doubting and so of the 'ordre
des raisons' in which it is 'le premier principe' (4,1: 34).

Thus the *cogito* is not a mere 'fact' offered perhaps as a
'proof' of Descartes's existence. It is not, in spite of the 'donc',
a deduction or an inference. It is not a claim to necessary
existence, nor is it a *tautology. It is not, in spite of the dramatic
presentation in Part 4, the first principle of an *a priorism*, a

premise from which all other truths follow, the ultimate truth upon which all knowledge is based. Still less is it a foundation for philosophical *idealism. The *cogito* is a mental intuition involving a movement of thought, a logical implication. It is a 'proposition simple', a necessary truth which is true each time Descartes, in one, immediate act of self-awareness, grasps the relationship between his thought and his existence; he necessarily exists if and while he thinks (4,3: 55-58). And the *cogito* is 'le premier principe de la philosophie' (4,1: 34) because it is 'la première et la plus certaine [conclusion] qui se présente à celui qui conduit ses pensées par ordre' (*1*, IX, p.27); general notions being discovered through and in particular intuitions, 'whatever thinks is' is discovered in the *cogito* itself (*2*, p.4). And the *cogito* is presupposed whenever we think of anything, because to be aware of something is at the same time to be aware of oneself (*2*, p.7). The *cogito* shows that the mind, without the help of the senses or of the imagination, is capable of a truth that bears on reality. It gives Descartes a toehold on Being but, at this stage in the 'ordre des raisons', no more. What matters for Descartes is not the *cogito* itself, but what he can do with it, what is implicit in it, what it can generate, and this can be revealed only in further analysis.

The 'très grande utilité' (*1*, IX, p.9) of the *cogito* lies firstly in the fact that 'ce biais est tout le meilleur...pour connaître la nature de l'âme, et qu'elle est une substance entièrement distincte du corps' (*1*, IX, p.28). By the *cogito* one knows that the self is 'une substance dont toute l'essence ou la nature n'est que de penser...en sorte que ce moi, c'est-à-dire l'âme...est entièrement distincte du corps' (4,2: 45-49). This 'moi', or 'âme', or 'être', is 'la première chose qu'on puisse connaître certainement' (*1*, I, p.353), and is therefore, in the 'ordre des raisons', easier to know than the body (4,2: 49-50). It is capable of existing without the body (4,1: 50-51), and is therefore really, and not simply conceptually, distinct from it (*1*, IX, p.131).

Here we have what Descartes admitted was an obscure account of the transition from the purely instantaneous awareness of oneself doubting and existing only as long as one doubts, to the assertion of an entity, a soul, 'une chose qui pense, c'est-à-dire un esprit, un entendement ou une raison' (*1*, IX, p.21). The importance of this transition is that it prepares the way for the dualism of 'pensée' and 'étendue' (respectively the main attributes, or 'essences', or 'natures', of incorporeal and corporeal substance) — the so-called Cartesian dualism apparently so advantageous to both religion and science. 'Pensée', all that was 'subjective' and 'inner', was a separate complete substance (for the Scholastics the soul was, like the body, an incomplete substance and had animal and vegetative functions), both mind and soul (terms with different though related meanings in Scholastic philosophy) and so a stronger candidate for immortality. And, as a separate substance exhaustively known as 'étendue', matter was devoid of the animistic properties attributed to it by the Scholastics, and was fully knowable by mathematical physics alone. How are we to understand Descartes's momentous transition (see below, pp.79-80) from thinking — 'je pense' — to thought —'une chose qui pense'?

It is helpful to bear in mind two things here: the 'ordre des raisons' and Descartes's somewhat obscure doctrine of essences or 'natures simples'. The *cogito* asserts as indubitable the existence of 'quelque chose', a 'moi' (4,1: 29) of some sort (the possibility of thought without a subject being excluded — see above, pp.53-54) but, in the 'ordre des raisons', this vague notion must give way to a clear and distinct notion of the essence of the self. What matters is not that I am, but what I am, what this 'moi', in so far as I doubt, is. Doubt of the existence of the body has led to the certainty of his own existence: he can know that he is 'thinking' (in his broad sense of the word) without knowing anything at all about his body. Therefore, that of which he is certain at this stage in his enquiry is only the existence of his mind/consciousness/soul/understanding/reason/will (and therefore freedom) — 'pensée'. Such immediate subjective awareness is uniquely certain precisely because it is immediate; the body is known 'mediately' through the soul. What Descartes believes he has discovered then is a 'nature simple', thinking substance, which, because it is simple, cannot be bodily: 'De cela seul qu'on conçoit clairement et distinctement les deux natures

de l'âme et du corps comme diverses, on connaît que
véritablement elles sont diverses, et par conséquent que l'âme
peut penser sans le corps' (*I*, II, p.38).

The second 'très grande utilité' (see above, p.54) of the *cogito*
was that within it lay the criterion of truth of any
proposition:'les choses que nous concevons fort clairement et
fort distinctement sont toutes vraies' (4,3: 59-60). For, in the
'ordre des raisons', it is reflection on the nature of the primary
truth, the *cogito*, that leads to the formulation of the 'règle'
which then serves to measure, to enable us to recognise, all other
truths. Thus the *cogito*, by virtue of its priority in the
metaphysical 'ordre des raisons', confirms the first rule of the
Method.

Having established the existence of 'l'âme séparée du corps'
(see above, p.49), Descartes now attempts to 'démontrer
l'existence de Dieu' in three elegant proofs. The first two,
'anthropological' and *a posteriori*, owe much to St Thomas
Aquinas, the third, *ontological and a priori*, to St Anselm, but
the way in which Descartes adapts these proofs to the 'ordre des
raisons' transforms them radically. The difficulty of these
proofs does not lie so much in their articulation as in their
presuppositions, not all of which are stated in Part 4, and many
of which may well appear strange to a modern reader: the 1637
reader was in the same position, but it is some measure of
Descartes's importance that, very often, what that reader found
familiar, we now find unfamiliar and what baffled him we now
tend to take for granted. Let us therefore look first at the
presuppositions of the first proof of God (4,4: 63-88).

4,4 shows that reflection on doubt generates the first proof,
but it is not made clear how Descartes's bold use of the principle
of causality has led to a new idea of God and to a new doctrine
of ideas — what is now known as representationalism (see below,
pp.79-80). To understand Descartes's thinking here we must
remember that doubt has not threatened our common notions,
of which the first is the principle of causality (see above, p.51).
'Il n'y a aucune chose existante de laquelle on ne puisse
demander quelle est la cause pourquoi elle existe [et] cela même
se peut demander de Dieu', who is not, as the Scholastics

thought, the uncaused First Cause, but Cause of Himself, *Causa sui*, in that 'l'immensité même de sa nature est la cause ou la raison pour laquelle il n'a besoin d'aucune chose pour exister' (*1*, IX, p.127). And one can ask that also of ideas.

Ideas 'represent' objects to the mind — objects which, at the stage of his enquiry in 4,4, he does not know to exist 'hors de moi' (line 70) — and thus give us indirect knowledge of the things 'represented' in the ideas. The 'representative nature' of an idea Descartes calls its 'réalité objective' and defines as 'l'entité ou l'être de la chose représentée par l'idée, en tant que cette entité est dans l'idée' (*1*, IX, p.124); things exist 'objectively', 'par représentation' (*1*, IX, p.106), in the ideas that 'represent' them. Having innovated by granting 'objective reality', 'objective being', to ideas, Descartes could now take the further step of applying the causal principle to this reality. Since 'toute la réalité ou perfection qui est dans une chose se rencontre formellement — [c'est-à-dire] d'une semblable façon — ou éminemment — [c'est-à-dire] d'une plus excellente façon — dans sa cause première et totale...il suit...que la réalité objective de nos idées requiert une cause, dans laquelle cette même réalité soit contenue...formellement ou éminemment'. Not to accept this axiom was to make all knowledge impossible (*1*, IX, pp.106, 128) — a justifiable claim from one whose starting point is methodical doubt and who must therefore move from ideas to things, from essences to existences. We must note too that the cause in question is total, not partial or a mere condition, and that, unlike much modern thought that divorces fact and value, Descartes holds that there are different degrees of reality, that 'il y a plus de réalité objective...dans l'idée de la substance infinie que dans l'idée de la substance finie' (*1*, IX, p.128) — a restatement of the Scholastic axiom that 'Ens et verum et bonum convertuntur' (Being, Truth and Goodness are interchangeable). Thus error is equivalent to non-being (4,4: 74-78).

The principle of causality is then the most important principle on which the first proof relies, but, as Gueroult argues (*23*, I, p.185), it needs to be supplemented by the principle of 'correspondance', which establishes that the idea of God 'se rapporte à quelque chose à quoi elle...soit...conforme' (*1*, IX, p.181), that is to say that it resembles its cause, that it is as it were the trademark 'mise en moi' (4,4: 84), 'imprimé[e]...en nos âmes' (5,1: 19-20) by the divine Workman, and not merely the result of God's action on our souls. And 'mise en moi' evokes an important metaphysical doctrine which is implicit in the *Discours* but was never expounded in any published work, the so-called theory of the creation of eternal truths (*1*, I, p.152), amongst which truths is to be found the idea of God.

This theory declared God to be the *efficient and total cause not only of all beings and things, but of essences. Rejecting the view that our knowledge was, in some sense, participation in God's knowledge, Descartes affirmed that God guaranteed the truth of our knowledge from, as it were, the outside. In this way Descartes achieved two apparently incompatible ends. On the one hand he increased the gulf between our knowledge and that of God: for He appeared even more transcendent and incomprehensible in His purposes, and our knowledge became the completely adequate knowledge of finite essences (2,9: 268-71). On the other he established a close relationship between God and human knowledge: for all our knowledge depended ultimately upon the guarantee of a veracious God who, free Creator of both the laws of nature and of the essences, the 'natures simples' in our minds (5,1: 18-20), has also created conformity between these laws and these essences and thus ensured the rationality of the universe. We can be certain that God is able to do all that we can understand, but we cannot, without presumption, say that He is unable to do what we cannot understand.

If one bears in mind these presuppositions, the first proof presents little difficulty. I doubt and am therefore imperfect (doubt being lack of truth and therefore lack of being), but I have the clear and distinct idea of something more perfect than myself, of 'un être plus parfait que le mien' (4,4: 67, 78-79). What is the total cause of this idea? Certainly, the cause must be as real (a 'formal' cause), or even more real (an 'eminent' cause), than the 'objective reality' of the idea, and I myself, as imperfect, cannot be such a cause. If then the clear and distinct idea — the clearest and most distinct of all our ideas — of 'un être plus parfait que le mien' cannot be a 'factitious' idea — one imagined by me — nor an 'adventitious' idea — one deriving from things 'hors de moi' (4,4: 70) — it must be an 'innate' idea (innate in the sense of virtual in the mind, of course, not of necessarily present). It must be an idea of which the content, an immutable and eternal essence, derives neither from the imagination nor from the senses, and which can only have been placed in me by a being whose nature is more perfect than mine and which has in itself all the perfections of which I can have any idea — God himself (4,4: 84-88). Therefore God exists and must exist.

This idea of God, Descartes stressed, was not born from the negation of the finite, but was a positive idea, because 'je vois manifestement qu'il se rencontre plus de réalité dans la substance infinie, que dans la substance finie, et partant que j'ai en quelque façon premièrement en moi la notion de l'infini, que du fini, c'est-à-dire de Dieu, que de moi-même' (*1*, IX, p.36) — 'en quelque façon', that is to say implicitly in the order of being, not explicitly in the 'ordre des raisons' (see above, p.50). And, Descartes could claim with some justification, the God thus discovered by moving from the clear and distinct idea of Him to His existence really was God, and not simply a First Cause as in Aquinas's proof of God based on His effects.

The second proof is offered 'non tant pour apporter une raison différente de la précédente [cf. 4,4: 88] que pour expliquer la même plus exactement' (*1*, IX, p.84), to bring out its implications: the imperfect being with the idea of the Perfect of which God is the cause depends totally for its existence upon the God who created it and gave it this idea. Thus Proof 1 finds the cause of the idea of God that is in Descartes's mind, Proof 2 the cause of Descartes who has this idea. And it is because Descartes finds the cause not simply of himself but of himself with the idea of God that his second proof is quite different from Aquinas's second proof from contingency and is able to make explicit 'toutes les perfections' (4,4: 98-99) of God which are contained in Descartes's idea of Him (4,4: 99-123). To understand this proof we must bear in mind the theory of the creation of eternal truths, the conception of God as *Causa sui*, and the principle of

causality: the cause must have as much 'formal' reality as there
is 'objective' reality in the effect. But we must note too that
Descartes accepts as self-evident the Scholastic view that the will
'naturally' seeks the good, that he holds the will to be infinite,
and that he presupposes his original doctrine of divine
continuous creation (alluded to in 4,4: 122-23) and the
discontinity of time, which doctrine takes up the traditional view
that 'l'action par laquelle [Dieu] conserve [le monde] est toute la
même que celle par laquelle il l'a créé' (5,4: 121-23). Thus 'il est
nécessaire que Dieu soit l'auteur de mon existence' refers to the
total and efficient cause that conserves him, a finite being
incapable of prolonging its existence from moment to moment,
in existence *now*, rather than to that cause as creator of his being
at birth (*I*, IX, p.39).

Proof 2 starts then from the same point as Proof 1 — an
imperfect being with the idea of a perfect being — but draws
from this contingent fact the conclusion that he cannot be the
author of his being and this idea. For, 'si j'avais la puissance de
me conserver moi-même, j'aurais aussi, à plus forte raison, le
pouvoir de me donner toutes les perfections qui me manquent'
and to which I aspire, just as God, as *Causa sui*, gives Himself
His perfections (*I*, IX, p.130). In fact I would be God — an
absurd hypothesis. Therefore, as an imperfect being with the
idea of a perfect being, I cannot give myself existence. Nor of
course can this existence come from any other (imperfect) being.
Therefore I must be maintained in existence by a being who has
'en soi formellement ou éminemment, tout ce qui est en moi' —
above all 'la notion de plusieurs perfections qui me manquent,
et...l'idée d'un Dieu' (loc. cit.). This being must be perfect and
therefore infinite and omnipotent (4,4: 97-98). He must be so
powerful that 'tout ce qui est en nous de réel et de vrai' (4,7: 202)
comes from Him as 'source de toute bonté et vérité' (*I*, IX,
p.35), that is to say as Creator of the eternal truths of which the
most important is the idea of Him which He has put into us (4,4:
84). Such a being can only be God. Therefore God exists and
must exist.

We now come to Descartes's last, ontological proof of the
existence of God, the proof of God from His essence. Offered as

a deepening of the two 'causal' proofs, it is really, as a consequence of the conception of God as *Causa sui*, a causal proof itself, and so very different from its medieval original. 4,5's presentation of this proof, basically that of the fifth *Méditation*, moves from the essence of material things, 'étendue' or spatial extension, to the idea of God by a route that often puzzles readers but is quite straightforward as long as its stages are discerned.

First Descartes distinguishes the clear and distinct ideas of extension, figure and number (4,5: 125-29) (guaranteed by the criterion of clear and distinct ideas (see above, p.56)) from the confused ideas of heat, colour and other sense impressions (4,4: 71) upon which Aristotelian physics was based, stressing that the former are 'innate' ideas, eternal truths discovered not made. 'All the demonstrations of mathematicians deal with true entities and objects', and the only difference between mathematics and physics is that the former 'considers its object merely as possible, i.e. as something which does not actually exist in space but is capable of doing so' (cf. 4,5: 134-35) and that physics — at this point in his enquiry still a distant possibility of course — 'considers its object not just as a true and real entity, but also as something actually and specifically existing' (*2*, p.23). The idea of a triangle is one such true and real entity, to which its properties belong necessarily (4,5: 136-37) and which is capable of existing in space (4,5: 137-39).

Now, the idea of God, of a Perfect Being, is also an innate idea, an essence discovered in the mind, in fact the clearest and most distinct of all one's ideas. But this idea is unique in a much more fundamental way. For whereas the essence of the triangle does not include necessary existence, the essence of the idea of God does. Were God to lack being, He would lack a perfection as necessary to His essence as the properties of a triangle are necessary to its essence (4,5: 141-42). And He would lack this perfection in the sense that He would lack — as Proof 2 showed Descartes himself to lack — the power to maintain Himself in being, that is to say, since God is *Causa sui* through the superabundance of His own nature, the power to give Himself existence. Therefore God exists and must exist — a metaphysical truth more certain than any mathematical truth (4,5: 144; cf. 5,2: 59-61).

Having demonstrated somewhat obscurely in Part 4 the real distinction of body and soul and the existence of God, Descartes now explains very obscurely how the veracity of God, which can be understood only in the context of the theory of the creation of eternal truths, guarantees both the criterion of clear and distinct ideas and the reality of the external world. He gives no guidance on how to distinguish between dreaming and wakefulness, between sense impressions and imagination, or, of course, between normal sense impressions and the delusions of madness (see below, p.65), and disrupts the 'ordre des raisons' with the result that the important elements of *theodicy in these arguments are obscured. Let us look first at the question of God's guarantee of the truth of clear and distinct ideas in its context and in the light of Descartes's later comments on this question in that context.

The main problem here is this: does 4,7: 186-90 involve Descartes in a vicious circle, the so-called Cartesian circle? That is to say, does Descartes not use his 'règle', the criterion of self-evidence, to prove the existence of God, and then use God to guarantee the truth of his 'règle'? This objection merits consideration not because, in my view, it is well founded, but because it is often advanced and because to answer it is to deepen one's understanding of the relationship in Descartes's thought between human knowledge and God. We must first examine more closely Descartes's conception of his 'règle' and of God.

'Règle' implies the discovery of the universal in the particular (see above, p.56). It is the natural light itself, 'la faculté de connaître que [Dieu] nous a donnée' and which, God not being a deceiver but the Perfect Being, cannot fail us providing we use it well; and this guarantee applies, with the same important restriction, not only to the understanding, but to the will (*1*, IX, p.43). This God is the *Causa sui* of the theory of the creation of eternal truths, a God who could, had He so desired — for He created both existences and essences — have created a quite different world with a quite different geometry and therefore with quite different clear and distinct ideas, but a God who cannot deceive or change His decrees, because such actions would betoken imperfection. All hangs on the beneficent omnipotence of this incomprehensible deity, whose existence is 'la première et la plus éternelle de toutes les vérités, et la scule d'où procèdent toutes les autres (*1*, I, p.150).

If God is the origin of truth (4,7: 201-03) what is the origin of error? It is this question, the subject matter of the fourth *Méditation*, that in Part 4 provides the context of the divine guarantee of clear and distinct ideas. The equivalence of truth and being once granted (see above, p.57), God's guarantee of truth is at the same time a guarantee that error is not from Him but from man. This is the ultimate, metaphysical explanation of the origins of truth and error, and 4,7 remains on this exalted level. However, Descartes's later explanation of 4,7: 201-05 does not, and helps us to understand why the Cartesian circle objection is misconceived.

We have seen that, on the purely practical level, error arises when we do not use our understanding and will 'well'. What exactly does this mean? According to Burman, Descartes told him that 'if we did not know that all truth has its origin in God [a reference to the theory of the creation of eternal truths], then however clear our ideas were, we would not know that they were true, or that we were not mistaken'. But he added: 'I mean of course when we were not paying attention to them, and when we merely remembered that we had clearly and distinctly perceived them. For on other occasions, when we do pay attention to the truths themselves, even though we may not know God exists, we cannot be in any doubt about them. Otherwise, we could not prove that God exists' (2, pp.49-50).

If we take these lines to reflect Descartes's 1637 metaphysics, 4,7 is concerned not only with the first cause — God — of the self-evidence of clear and distinct ideas, but also with the problem of the 'ordre des raisons' and whether 4,7 has violated it; 4,7 shows how the two orders, the explicit order of discovery or 'ordre des raisons' and the implicit order of being, ultimately come together. In the former, 'évidence' does not 'need' the divine guarantee while it is attended to, and the proposition that

God (the necessarily perfect and therefore veracious Being) exists can, Descartes claims at least, be established without, as it were, going outside this 'évidence'. Therefore in principle there is no circularity in argument. That one cannot acknowledge at a given, early stage in the 'ordre des raisons' that one's rational faculties depend on God does not prevent one from discovering later that they have done and that they do and must do; 'évidence' is now seen to have the divine guarantee, the implicit has become explicit.

This guarantee is seen to extend to all clearly and distinctly perceived ideas, whether present in the mind or not. 'Ces longues chaînes de raisons' (2,8: 215) are guaranteed, not because God guarantees our memory (!) or powers of enumeration, but because the God who created both essences and existences guarantees the conformity of human reason and natural law — the rationality of the universe. And this is why in 4,7 the lines 186 to 190 are preceded by a question (lines 180 to 183) which throws the consistency, and thus the order, of the universe into doubt. God conserves the continuity of the universe from (essentially discontinuous) moment to moment (see above, pp.59-60) and thus conserves rational truth from (instantaneous) 'évidence' to 'évidence'. Without God man would know a few disconnected truths, but not the truth — a systematic body of truth. He would know, for example, some mathematical truths, but not why the general certainty of mathematics is certain. He could never be sure that what seemed self-evident really was so, that some doubt would never come to him from some quarter. Thus he would never possess true, indubitable knowledge, 'science' in its full Cartesian sense. God, not any merely human truth, is 'le roc' (3,6: 174), the grounds upon which all human knowledge must be founded.

Finally, God's guarantee of the existence of the external world. In Part 4 a doubt of the external world that has to be presented ambiguously and obscurely leads quite naturally to what is no more than a sketch of a proof of the existence of that world (see above, pp.52-53). But there is another reason for this sketch I suspect. Having spent several paragraphs attacking 'naïve realism' — our natural inclination to believe that the

world is as it appears — and therefore the knowledge claims of
the senses and the imagination, Descartes could hardly explain,
as he was to in the sixth *Méditation*, that it was precisely in
God's guarantee of this natural inclination (provided it were
properly understood and kept within bounds) that the strongest
proof of the existence of the external world was to be found.
Such a paradoxical rehabilitation of the senses would have
confused the philosophically inept and blunted his point that it is
reason alone that gives us the essence of things (4,6: 164-66; 4,8:
221-23) and therefore that it is upon 'étendue' alone, not upon
the obscure ideas formed on the occasion of sense impressions,
that physics must be founded.

Nevertheless, if one reads 4,8: 230-35 carefully, and looks for
clues in the rest of Part 4, one glimpses the essential points made
in the sixth *Méditation*. Thus, Descartes had 'pensées' or 'des
idées de plusieurs choses sensibles et corporelles' (4,4: 69,
109-10) existing in space (4,5: 124-30), and knew that if, as the
understanding declared to be possible, these things existed, they
were of a different nature from 'pensée'. Why is it then that no
sane person (4,7: 174-75) can doubt that sense objects exist, that
we have a natural propensity to posit their existence
or, more accurately, an inability not to posit their existence —
and that this 'assurance morale' (4,7: 173) is fully valid on it own
level?

Descartes's paradoxical answer is basically that this is
precisely because sense impressions are so different from the self
as a thinking substance and have a 'givenness' about them that
cannot be willed away. Also, to doubt that 'toute idée doit avoir
une cause de sa réalité objective, qui soit réellement existante' is
to doubt the causal principle used to prove the existence of God
and to make all knowledge impossible (see above, p.57). If
however we want 'certitude métaphysique' (4,7: 176) on the
existence of the external world, we must find it in the veracity of
God, who could not have misled us on such an important
subject. On the contrary, as 'mises en nous' (4,8: 234-35)
suggests, Providence has given us these sense impressions for
our welfare, so that we can know what things are useful or
harmful to us. Thus the senses are usually reliable (4,1: 15-16)

and God has given us, and guaranteed, an instrument, reason, to correct them when necessary (4,8: 219-23); He is thus no more responsible for the errors of the senses than for the errors of reason. In effect, God has guaranteed human nature when it functions as He intended. On one level (or 'ordre' in the Pascalian sense) reason gives us the 'primary qualities' of things, their essence, things as they really are. On another level, the senses give us their 'secondary qualities', things as they appear to us in our everyday life. And there is no conflict between these levels, each of which is valid in its own way. The hope is now given that, if man avoids 'précipitation' and 'prévention', true knowledge, a 'science universelle', will be his.

5. Science and Scientific Method

In this chapter I shall discuss Descartes's account in Part 6 of his scientific method and how this method could have produced the scientific results outlined in Part 5. I shall then assess the importance of Descartes's physics (rather than discuss its largely outdated details) before examining Descartes's 'mechanical' treatment of living beings (including man), the questions of the union of the soul and body, of animal-machines and, finally, of the immortality of the soul — a metaphysical question which Descartes nevertheless places in Part 5. Why he did this will become clear when, to conclude this chapter, I look at what the *Discours* has to tell us on the implications of his science for certain Catholic beliefs of his day.

What is the nature of Descartes's scientific method? The Method involves the training of 'esprit' as a whole, not simply of the intellect, which must be 'aidé' in mathematics by the imagination, and in physics by the senses (*1*, X, pp.410-11) — by 'expérience' in both its seventeenth-century senses of 'observation' and 'experiment'. Thus Descartes insists both that his principles are 'très simples et très évidents' (6,6: 291-92; cf. 6,4: 209-12) and that their success is inevitable only if he can make numerous experiments and observations (6,2: 77-80). These have an important role to play at all stages of scientific enquiry: experience gives us facts which have to be 'explained', i.e. deduced from general principles, and these principles are 'proved' by their being shown to be consistent with the facts (6,10: 426-34).

Thus Descartes's scientific method is no mere *deductivism. Nor is it, as Pascal's was, 'hypothetical-deductive', for though it uses experiments to discover which of several, hypothetical mechanisms is the true one, it does not regard that true hypothesis as subject to falsification by further experiment. Nor, in spite of its borrowings from Bacon is it *inductive, for

though the 'natures simples', 'étendue', 'figure' and 'mouvement', on which it is based are elicited on the occasion of sense
experience, they, and *a fortiori* the laws of physics as a whole,
cannot be 'derived' from experience. It is indeed unique, a
specific application of a general Method rooted in metaphysics.

The first stage in this scientific method is laid down in 6,3:
101-06. These lines remind the researcher that reason alone,
guaranteed by God, the Creator of eternal truths, of 'natures
simples' (6,3: 105-06) and of the laws of nature (5,1: 18-20), can
tell him what constitutes an explanation in physics, and so tell
him what to look for in nature. Explanation must be 'reductive'
— reducing everything to what Newton's *Principia* called 'the
universal qualities of all bodies whatever', in Descartes's case
the 'natures simples' 'figure', 'étendue' and 'mouvement' —
and 'mechanical' — using no other principles of explanation
than those used in mechanics and therefore seeing nature as a
machine with moving parts and only as this.

However, unaided reason tells the researcher only what is
possible in the outside world, it does not tell him what things
God has created or what their 'dimensions' — length, breadth,
weight, speed — are. Nor does it tell him which of many possible
mechanisms God has chosen in any given case. Thus reason
alone cannot give man mastery over nature (6,3: 118; cf. 6,2:
55-56). True, a large number of easily observable phenomena
can be easily explained by Descartes's principles (6,3: 106-12).
And Descartes warns against the sort of fascination with
unusual occurrences (6,3: 93-100) to which Bacon had
succumbed in his own work on method, the *Novum Organum*.
But, as research proceeds, reason must be aided more and more
by, and in this sense is more and more dependent upon,
observation and experiment in order to 'distinguer les formes ou
espèces de corps qui sont sur la terre d'une infinité d'autres qui
pourraient y être' (6,3: 115-17). Indeed, 'la puissance de la
nature est si ample et si vaste', and Descartes's principles 'si
simples et si généraux', that the researcher will find hardly any
particular effect that cannot be deduced from them in several
different ways, which he must therefore enumerate. And to find
in which way an effect depends on these principles he must

conduct experiments 'qui soient telles, que leur événement ne soit pas le même, si c'est en l'une de ces façons qu'on doit l'expliquer, que si c'est en l'autre' (6,3: 124-33) — a Cartesian adaptation of Bacon's 'crucial experiment'.

What is the worth of this theory of scientific research? Descartes wished his Method to be judged by its 'fruits' (1,3: 38) and, in 1637 and in the scientific field, these were primarily the *essais* (6,9: 402), but also the 'quelque chose de...physique et de médecine' in Part 5, which shows that the Method 's'étend à toutes sortes de matières' (*1*, I, p.349). What then is the nature of Cartesian science? Is is 'genuine' science or not?

Certainly, the *essais* contain much that justifies Descartes's confidence in them. The *Géométrie* did 'demonstrate' (*1*, I, p.478) the superiority of the Method by proposing an analytical geometry that founded modern mathematics and that was eventually to prove, along with the calculus, the indispensable tool of the new science in that it enabled scientists to define space mathematically. And the *Dioptrique*, on the whole, could 'persuade' (loc. cit.) readers of the Method's superiority by embodying that combination of reason and experiment advocated in 6,3 in order to give a theoretical deduction of the sine law of the refraction of light, to explain the action of the eye and, most of all (6.11: 455-63), to show how lens-grinding, essential to the development of the microscope, could be improved. As for *Discours* 8 of the *Météores*, this contains the first complete account of the formation of the primary and secondary bow of the rainbow, and one that is still regarded as a model of scientific method — which was how Descartes himself saw this *Discours*.

There seems little doubt then that Descartes's Method could produce genuine scientific 'fruits', valuable contributions to the development of Classical Physics. And, according to Part 6, only factors which hindered experimentation — lack of time (6,2: 79-80), of money, of manual skill (6,3: 137), and of competent fellow scientists (6,7: 335-52) — prevented Descartes from making more such contributions. This situation could only get worse as experiments became more difficult (6,6: 311-14) and more numerous (6,3: 136-37).

Now, these factors were real enough, and it was true that the times were not favourable to the hierarchical organisation of scientific research which alone could ensure the rapid development of the new science that Descartes, Bacon and other innovators desired. But these factors help to explain what Descartes has not done, rather than what he has done. They do not explain adequately why most of Descartes's science is not of this genuine, quantitative type, but exhibits the tendency to be more interested in elaborating a unified theory than in establishing particular facts, to see the explanation of all natural phenomena by the positing of plausible mechanisms as more important than the discovery of new facts through experimentation and so, paradoxically, to be content with merely qualitative and therefore inexact description.

This tendency, much present in the *Météores*, shows in Descartes's 'mechanical' explanation of the movement of the heart (see below, pp.73-74)). Here (5,6 to 5,9) he makes a powerful and scientifically valuable plea for observation and experiment — for he was an enthusiastic dissector — and for a purely mechanist physiology. But he is uncritical towards sense experience, and therefore falls into scientific error, precisely because of his overriding concern to promote his consistent mechanism (one applicable to both living and inanimate things) by showing the Scholastics that his explanation is better than theirs since it is of the correct 'mechanical' type, and by showing Harvey that it is better than his because it is more, in fact entirely, 'mechanical' (whereas Descartes used the analogy of the kettle, Harvey used that of the pump and therefore, Descartes thought, attributed to the heart an 'occult' property of self-movement).

However, this tendency is epitomised by the sketch (5,1 to 5,3) of *Le Monde*'s grandiose account of the origin and nature of material things. Here we have a qualitative 'tableau' (5,2: 33), in Perrault's words a 'roman philosophique' with little quantitative content (and that incorrect), that Newton condemned as fanciful and untestable assumption and therefore not science at all, and that many detractors compared to the *De rerum natura* of Lucretius. How are we to explain that this 'tableau' was as much a 'fruit' of the Method as the *Géométrie* and that Descartes never created a system of the world of the precise, mathematical, Newtonian type, one that would allow scientific prediction and so make men 'comme maîtres et possesseurs de la Nature' (6,2: 55-56)?

A tentative answer to these difficult and much debated questions is that Descartes produced a qualitative 'tableau' because, believing (rightly) that that was all the Method could produce, he therefore believed (wrongly) that that was all human reason could produce. The Method sought 'toutes les choses, qui peuvent tomber sous la connaissance des hommes' and what it could not analyse could not be known by reason (2,8: 215-220; cf. 2,9: 265-78; 3,6: 174-81). What could be known in physics had first to be analysed mathematically, and Descartes's pre-calculus mathematics was not equal to the Newtonian task. Without an adequate mathematical tool, the researcher was thus in a paradoxical position. On the one hand, he had a clear and distinct idea of the nature of matter as 'une substance étendue en longueur, largeur et profondeur' (*1*, IX, p.65) and so knew more than Newton claimed to know or wished to know (his 'mass' is not the 'essence' of bodies and, as Gaukroger points out, 'the actual extension of bodies is irrelevant to their dynamical properties' (*20*, p.135). On the other, he knew much less than Newton claimed to know because, paradoxically enough for a 'rationalist', he was dependent upon experience to tell him which possible things and mechanisms actually existed — experience which could provide only probable, and therefore uncertain results, uncertain knowledge of an infinitely complex universe. Thus the researcher could discover a number of 'lois très générales comme les règles du mouvement [not divulged in the *Discours*], ou...un petit nombre de lois très particulières, comme celles de la réfraction' (*28*, p.201) but then had to content himself with a 'mechanical' description of how things are.

However, to judge the Method harshly for having produced a 'fruit' that is not precise science would be to be guilty of anachronism, for the nascent Scientific Revolution, as much — or more — a new way of explaining old facts as a new way of discovering new facts, needed both the piecemeal approach of Galileo and the imaginative, if scientifically premature, systemising of Descartes, who was attempting to provide (to use modern terminology) a philosophy, a philosophy of science, and a science. The Frenchman's greatest contribution to this Revolution was not his analytical geometry, whose worth was not appreciated until the end of the century, but to have established a 'mechanical' framework within which scientific advance could take place, a complete system of the universe that could replace that of Aristotle partly because it was of the same qualitative type and partly because it had a new 'mechanical' content, a system that held up the ideal — for the reality was not yet realisable — of the oneness of knowledge, of the interconnectedness of the sciences (5,1: 1-2), and of a mathematical physics.

Thus, for the first time since Antiquity all heavenly and earthly phenomena had been explained by recourse to a small number of laws, and a world-picture had appeared that was superior to any, existing or defunct, in three interdependent respects: it was simple (5,2: 61-65), because its explanation of things was reductive and therefore economical; it was readily graspable by common sense (6,10: 445-50), because based on the analogy between machines and natural phenomena (6,2: 48-55; the only difference between the two is that the mechanisms of the former are larger and therefore easier to perceive); and it was intelligible (5,2: 59-60), because 'étendue' was a clear and distinct idea that destroyed the epistemological roots of both Aristotelian science and Renaissance pseudo-science.

For, in Descartes's system of the universe, things no longer possessed, as the Scholastics thought, the qualities of dryness, heat, etc., or the 'substantial forms', the specific and irreducible essences that, supposedly, make them what they are (5,2: 62-63), or, if living, any 'âme végétante ou sensitive' (5,5: 145; the 'vegetative soul', common to all living things, plants, animals and men, governed nutrition and growth, the 'sensitive soul', common to animals and men, governed sensation and locomotion). Nor were there any mysterious or occult 'sympathies' between things as the so-called naturalism of the

Renaissance had thought and Fludd, for example, still thought: Descartes's clockwork universe swept away all such naïve anthropomorphism.

Its epistemological roots thus destroyed, Scholastic science must die. If God's purposes are unknown to us (see above, p.58) *final causes may be excluded from science, nature is no longer to be conceived as *teleological. If 'étendue' is a homogeneous 'corps continu' (4,5: 126; which, of course, excludes the possibility of the vacuum, soon to be established experimentally by Torricelli); if it is 'indéfiniment' extended (loc. cit.; i.e. we can conceive no boundary to it; God alone is 'infini' as this is a purely positive concept); and if its corpuscles are divisible to infinity (4,5: 127 expresses Descartes's concern to avoid possible theological objections), then it follows that there is no longer any distinction between a 'corruptible' sublunary world and an 'incorruptible' celestial realm, that the world, no longer finite, has no centre, and thus that nature is no longer hierarchical. Such a universe calls for a method that takes mathematics, not biology, for its model; that asks not what a thing does in its 'natural', i.e. hierarchical context, but what it would do in every conceivable context, and is therefore ready to consider ideal states; and that breaks down the distinction between mechanics, seen as the science of 'violent' man-made motion, and physics, seen as the science of 'natural' motion.

Thus, by what we would categorise more readily as a mechanical philosophy or as a philosophical mechanism than as a scientific mechanism, Descartes had in *Le Monde* turned men's minds in the direction in which alone scientific advance was possible. However — and not surprisingly, as it was unwise to banish final causes from biology — Descartes found the 'mechanical' explanation of the formation of living things much more difficult than that of inanimate things. As far as men and animals were concerned, he first supposed, in what was to become the 1664 *Traité de l'homme*, a man exhaustively describable in mechanistic terms, a body without its 'âme raisonnable' (5,5: 144) in which God had kindled 'un de ces feux sans lumière' (5,5: 146) which Descartes identified with life itself. In this body could only be all those functions which man shares with the animals, functions not 'dépendantes de la pensée' (5,5: 158) and therefore (see above, p.45 and pp.55-56) not willed (5,10: 402) and free, but determined by 'la seule disposition des organes' (5,7: 255). For the animal, and man in his involuntary processes, is 'une machine...faite des mains de Dieu' (5,10: 408-09), a machine in which the blood's heat is the ultimate cause of all involuntary processes (5,6: 163-65) in man and of all processes whatsoever in animals. Physical laws explain not only locomotion (5,9: 362-67), but also waking, sleeping, dreaming (5,10: 388-89), and perception itself as a causal process in which the animal spirits (5,9: 362-80) flow from the sense organs to the brain, where their sense impressions are retained (5,10: 394-95).

When one considers to what extent Descartes makes man a machine, a creature of reflexes and conditioned reflexes, one understands how he could see 'imagining' (5,13: 504) that animals are any more than machines as the most tenacious childhood prejudice. A man who had never seen an animal, but had the mechanical knowledge and the skill to make 'automates, ou machines mouvantes' (5,10: 403-04) in the form of animals and men, would, when he saw animals for the first time, and 'principalement s'il était imbu de la connaissance de Dieu', judge that they were simply machines made by an infinitely more skilful Workman, God Himself (*1*, II, pp.39-41; cf. 5,10: 402-12). And he would judge rightly, for, since art imitates nature (an Aristotelian notion) and men can make 'automates', it is reasonable to suppose that nature makes them too but better (*1*, V, pp.277-78). Recognising by experience that Man was more than his own manlike 'automates', this man would recognise *ipso facto* that Man is more than an animal and would express this difference in terms of Cartesian dualism: animals lack 'raison' (5,11: 415), 'connaissance' (5,11: 437), thought (5,11: 424), 'âme' (5,12: 471), 'esprit' (5,12: 484), that is to say, 'pensée'. For, Descartes argues, experience provides two 'moyens très certains' (5,11: 420) of distinguishing between men and animals, the criteria of language and versatility.

By language, the 'true difference' between men and animals (*1*, V, pp.277-78), Descartes understands 'paroles' or 'd'autres signes' (5,11: 423; e.g. deaf and dumb language, 5,12: 457-58) composed or arranged 'diversement' (5,11: 431) to respond appositely to what is said or asked and not haphazardly or simply as a result of a given stimulus or conditioned reflex (5,11: 424-30; 5,12: 454-57). The fact that even madmen (5,12: 448) are capable of doing this but that no animal can, proves *a fortiori*, Descartes believed, that there is a qualitative, unbridgeable gulf between men and animals. The second criterion concerns men's non-linguistic acts, which show reason to be 'un instrument universel' (5,11: 438). Even 'un enfant des plus stupides' (5,12: 469-70) shows more adaptability than any animal or (the two being identified) machine, whose actions depend on the disposition of their organs or parts. And, Descartes assumes, no machine can be made that will imitate human versatility...

Mechanism, based on the clear and distinct idea of 'étendue' and appealing to experience, having adequately explained animal behaviour, the onus is upon Descartes's Montaigne-reading opponents to prove that animals are more than machines. And this they could not do (they could not point to machines that now reproduce human speech (5,11: 424-33) — a double-edged argument this, of course — or to animals that now have been taught a very simplified language). To claim for example that we simply do not understand animal language (5,12: 474-76) is to invite the reply that 'comme les chiens [etc.] nous expriment leurs passions, ils nous exprimeraient aussi bien leurs pensées, s'ils en avaient' (*1*, IV, p.575; cf. 5,12: 476-78). And that various species, for example bees, 'témoignent plus d'industrie [= skill] que nous en quelques-unes de leurs actions' merely proves that they are like any clock, which tells the time more accurately than any human can (5,12: 480-90). However, Descartes does not, and cannot, claim more than the highest probability for the thesis of animal-machines, for he cannot prove that God has not joined 'quelque [indiscernable] pensée' to animal organs (*1*, IV, p.576). And, we might add, it is of the nature of categorial frameworks, of Cartesian dualism and of its rivals, that they are not susceptible of absolute proof.

So much then for animals. But man is more than a machine, God has given him an 'âme raisonnable' (5,5: 144), 'la seule chose qui nous rend hommes, et nous distingue des bêtes' (1,2:

25-26) — the voluntary processes, functions 'dépendantes de la pensée' (5,5: 158), that give man his freedom and dignity. For man is both 'étendue' and 'pensée', two independent and complete substances. No combination of 'figure' and 'mouvement' could have produced 'pensée', which must therefore have been created especially by God (5,13: 491-94), and no action of 'pensée' can change the amount of motion in the material world, since God keeps this amount constant (a physical 'principe' the *Discours* could not mention). How then can man be a unitary being, and how can two such heterogeneous substances interact?

Descartes's answer to these questions is to present the real, substantial union of body and mind as a fact for which the main evidence is our experience of their interaction. Were the soul not 'jointe et unie...étroitement' with the body, we would not have the 'sentiments' and 'appétits' we do, we would not be 'un vrai homme' at all (5,13: 497-99). This substantial union is a 'notion primitive' like 'étendue' and 'pensée', which is known only 'obscurément' by the pure understanding but 'très clairement par les sens' — which is why 'ceux qui ne philosophent jamais' do not doubt it for one moment (*1*, III, pp. 691-92). Here, and not in physics, final causes find their rightful place (see above, pp.65-66). Thus there is no philosophical problem of interaction and it is for science to explain what happens in the body when mental acts take place, what conditions must apply in the body for interaction to take place at all — to show, for example, that the soul can change the direction of the motion of the animal spirits (5,9: 370) if not add to the amount of this motion, and so act upon the body from its seat in the pineal gland.

Finally, the implications of Descartes's science (by which we mean principally *Le Monde*) for certain Catholic beliefs of his day. What were the main religious difficulties for Descartes's science, the 'quelques considérations' that prevented the publication of *Le Monde* (5,2: 27)?

Clearly, the Church, wedded to Aristotelianism, could only mistrust a physics that replaced and treated with irony the Aristotelian physics on which the current proofs of God were based and that refuted the Aristotelian explanation of transubstantiation. And then as now there were many defenders of orthodoxy who equated refuting the current arguments for a given belief with refuting that belief itself. Furthermore, in at least three respects, Descartes's science contradicted the Church's understanding of scripture: his *cosmogony contradicted Genesis on the order of creation and its nature, positing evolution rather than a six day creation; his astronomy contradicted the *geocentrism implied by, for example Joshua 10.12-13, in favour of heliocentrism (the *Discours*, prudently, only hints at this difficulty, 6,1: 6-8); his thesis of animal-machines contradicted many passages (e.g. Numbers 22. 28,30) which implied that animals had intelligence. What then could Descartes do in the *Discours* to make his science acceptable to the Church?

In the first place, unable either openly to embrace Copernican heliocentrism (6,1: 1-19) or to withhold all details of his cosmogony, Descartes resorted to the device of the 'fable '(*I*, I, p.179; cf. 1,5: 68) of 'un nouveau' (5,2: 50-51) possible world created from a state of chaos (5,2: 54) equally created by God. This 'fable' agreed, on the whole, with the Genesis account of the order of creation (Descartes's mechanist theory of light as a flow of particles from bodies could not be reconciled with Genesis as it demanded that sun, moon and stars pre-exist light in order to emit it). Descartes is careful to present his evolutionary, genetic account of creation as a requirement of theory (5,4: 130-32) rather than as the more 'probable' view (5,4: 116-20), the view that concords with the Church's understanding of Genesis. But at the same time he points out that his account is no less compatible with God's perfections than the traditional one, and that creation and conservation are for God one action (5,4: 120-30; see above, pp.59-60). Descartes could not in the *Discours* say in any clearer way that for him (in 1637 at least, for his later attitude is less clear) his 'possible' world was the real world and that, as Galileo thought too, the Genesis account should be interpreted allegorically.

In the second place, Descartes stressed the many advantages his science offered to religion (see above, pp.54-55). He is concerned to show above all that the animal-machine thesis

(5,10 to 5,12), apparently destructive of belief in human spirituality, in fact provided the strongest auxiliary proof of the immortality of the soul (5,13: 507-11). For Descartes, the Scholastics' projection of human spirituality onto animals engendered the inference, dangerous to virtue (5,13: 501-07), that animals have immortal souls — an inference that, since 'il n'y a point de raison pour le croire de quelques animaux, sans le croire de tous', leads to the absurd consequence of opening the gates of Heaven to the most 'imparfaits' (*1*, IV, p.576), to 'les mouches et les fourmis' (5,13: 507). Consistent mechanism on the other hand (supported elsewhere by judicious scriptural quotation, e.g. Leviticus 17.14) makes it easier to understand the metaphysical reasons that prove that the human soul is an independent, complete, immaterial substance, not subject to corruption or death, either through its own nature or through any purely natural exterior factor (5,13: 507-13), but only through an external supernatural factor, the will of God, who, having created and conserved it, could destroy it if He so wished.

Thus Cartesian metaphysics, though superior here to the Scholastics', can provide us only with a conditional certainty, a possible, not a certain proof, and it is revelation that gives us absolute certainty that the soul is immortal. Furthermore, consistent mechanism, by suppressing supposed animal 'souls' (the Introduction, 5,12: 471 and 5, 13: 504-05, 507-08 express Descartes's concern to avoid shocking his readers by stating this bold view too starkly), contributes to theodicy; for were it true that animals, who have not sinned, could suffer pain as we do, God would be unjust. In all, mechanism, by showing the 'immenses espaces' (5,3: 81) of the universe to be subject to a few simple laws 'établies' by God (5,2: 57), was the true Christian world-view, respectful of God's transcendence and wisdom, and a strong stimulus to piety. Such was the view of all seventeenth-century 'mechanical philosophers'. Descartes was simply bolder and more consistent than they, and therefore suspect to many who held the faith for which he was attempting to provide the form of philosophical expression appropriate to the new age.

Conclusion

The importance of the *Discours* lies in its open-ended and question-raising nature. It is, in the first place, an account of work in progress which presents us not with a completed and therefore closed system, but with an individual fighting for truth. However outmoded some of its ideas may be, the *Discours*'s stimulating and untechnical presentation of these ideas has always interested and inspired its readers, whether they be of a literary or a philosophical bent, and will do so as long as the search for truth is a prized human activity. Secondly, precisely because the *Discours* is allusive, elliptic, and sometimes even contradictory, a heterogeneous work aimed at several different audiences and which has several aims, it raises in an acute form the ever-debated question of the nature of Cartesian thought.

On the one hand the *Discours* presents us with the man whose work was in the 1660s and 1670s condemned by both Church and State, and points to what is 'this-worldly' in his thought and thus at the origins of our 'secularised' forward-looking technological civilisation. In Part 2 it presents us with four apparently anodine rules, as revolutionary and epoch-making as Marx's equally brief *Theses on Feuerbach* which were to challenge them with a new dialectical conception of reason. These rules are orientated towards self-mastery and mastery over the world, and point to a new conception of reason, of man, and of civilisation. In Part 6 it prophesies the new science, introduces some of its 'fruits' (the *essais*), sketches its method of reason allied to experiment, inspires us with the vision of a peaceful humanitarian science which is of ever-increasing relevance, and evokes a philosophy/wisdom that looks principally to medicine for the improvement of mankind. In Part 5 it establishes the 'mechanical' framework — what Marx called Descartes's 'engineer's view of reality' — within which this science was to evolve for two centuries, one which involved the classical (and now challenged) distinction between man's voluntary and involuntary processes, and gave Western thought an impulsion towards the search for universal laws from which a picture of the world could be obtained by pure deduction — Einstein's dream, now being realised. In Part 4 it establishes a dualism which raises serious philosophical difficulties but which is still the working hypothesis of most scientists: 'psychophysical dualism' — reality is bifurcated into two mutually exclusive worlds, the world of thought and the world of matter — and 'epistemological dualism' or 'representationalism' — reality is grasped only in 'ideas' which 'represent' it and which, as it were, interpose themselves between the knower and that reality. And Part 4 shows Descartes to be the father of both modern philosophies and of modern philosophy in its characteristic modes of thought. For Descartes's critical epistemology makes questions like 'how do I know?', 'can I be certain?', the first questions of all philosophy.

On the other hand, the *Discours* presents the man whose metaphysics was taken up by Christian thinkers as a tool of faith, and reveals the moral and religious framework within which these 'this-worldly' ideas have their being. It shows the moral/religious motivation of Descartes's 'philosophie... pratique' (6,2: 49-50), the crucial importance of the proofs of God in his metaphysics, the way in which this metaphysics continues the medieval 'perennial philosophy' (Leibnitz's phrase) of degrees of reality, of 'Ens, et bonum et verum convertuntur'. And it shows the constant apologetic concern that places him within the current of the Catholic Counter-Reformation.

However, open-endedness is not total inconclusiveness, and the reason why the *Discours* is a valuable introduction to Descartes's philosophy/science as a whole is that it raises the right questions for the understanding of his thought, questions which can be answered only by reference to later works. By showing us how what was to become Cartesianism arose not from the realm of abstractions (1,14: 221-22) but from an individual's experience in a particular social, religious, philosophical and scientific context in which European thought, we can now see, took a new direction, the *Discours* precludes any simplistic 'either/or' or 'unidirectional' interpretation of Descartes's thought. It invites us instead, in Pascal's phrase, to 'accorder tous les [perhaps purely apparent] contraires', to understand Descartes's enterprise as an attempt, inevitably not without its inner tensions, to synthesise what was most vital in that context — the new rationalism and religious faith — and so to erect a new Christian humanism.

Thus the *Discours* precludes our seeing Descartes simply as a defender of the faith or as a man who merely 'used' God to found a scientific humanism. It discourages our seeing Descartes's thought merely as an uneasy compromise between reason and faith in which dualism is but a device on the part of a scientist to avoid future 'demarcation disputes' between science and religion. Such unidirectional interpretations, by reading back later developments of Descartes's thought into his works, confuse the latter with the former, and sometimes go as far as to make Descartes solely responsible for the nature of modern Western thought, the better to condemn both.

The *Discours*, then, invites us to explore the close relationship which, for all Descartes's prudence vis-à-vis the theologians, it establishes between the natural and the supernatural, reason and faith, science and religion. It invites us to ask whether, or to what extent, Descartes's attempted synthesis of faith and reason was successful. It leads us to ask, for example, whether Descartes's thought, which constantly subordinates the natural to the supernatural in a way that has the effect, intentional or not, of widening the gap between the two (e.g. the use of the phrase 'en cette vie' (see above, pp.24-25), the dualism of 'pensée' and 'étendue' (see above, pp.54-55), and the theory of the creation of eternal truths (see above, p.58)) is to be understood, as Laporte thought, as a 'pluralisme cohérent' with 'oppositions' but not 'contradictions' (*28*, p.477). Or perhaps, is Descartes's thought as a whole subtly predetermined by his scientific preoccupations in that his very notion of reason, of method, expresses what Pascal called 'l'esprit de géometrie' and that this is responsible both for the order (as he claimed (*1*, IX, p.9)) *and* the distinctive doctrines of the metaphysics, the universal principle of efficient causation he had used in his science now being applied to both ideas, suitably redefined, and to God Himself, now seen as *Causa sui*? Whatever one's reply to such questions, to attempt to answer them is to understand better not only Descartes but oneself as a member of the civilisation he helped to shape, and to shape most dramatically, at least on the level of the non-specialist, by the *Discours* itself.

Glossary

This is a list not of definitions alone but of definitions and of notes which include definitions where, and to the extent, appropriate. (O.E.D. = *The Concise Oxford English Dictionary*)

A fortiori   With stronger reason, more conclusively (*O.E.D.*). An example of an *a fortiori* argument is: 'if A is stronger than B and if B can lift this weight, then, *a fortiori*, A can'.

A posteriori   Reasoning from effects to causes.

A priori   Reasoning from cause to effect; reasoning from what is held to precede and condition experience, e.g. from first principles.

Aristotelianism This was, largely in its Thomist form (i.e. 'christianised' by St Thomas Aquinas), the major philosophical component of *Scholasticism* (see below).

Contingency   What need not, may or may not, occur. The opposite of 'necessity'.

Cosmogony   Theory of the creation of the universe (*O.E.D.*).

Deductivism   A philosophy or method that, excluding experience, uses only deduction.

Dualism   The *metaphysical* (see below) theory that reduces reality to two basic substances not, e.g., to one (Monism) or to many (Pluralism).

Efficient cause The act or event that produces a given result.

Empiricism   The theory that all knowledge is derived from experience. Thus empiricism is opposed to Descartes's theory of innate ideas — an aspect of his '*rationalism*' (see below). In a looser sense of the term, an 'empirical' statement is a factual statement.

Epistemology   The theory of knowledge, what it is and how we attain it.

Final cause   The purpose for which something is made (see below, *teleological*).

Geocentrism   The theory that the earth is the centre of the universe.

Heliocentrism   The theory that the sun is the centre of the universe

Idealism   Philosophical idealism is the theory that only minds and their ideas exist.

Induction   Inductive reasoning infers a general conclusion from a number of instances and is the method of *empirical* (see above) generalisation.

Metaphysics   Metaphysics investigates philosophical matters which lie outside the range of *empirical* (see above) investigation. Traditionally, metaphysics has included *epistemology* (see above), *ontology* (see below) and cosmology.

Ontology   The *metaphysical* (see above) enquiry into being as such, i.e. not into the nature of any particular existent.

Rationalism   This is often defined against *empiricism* (see above) to mean the view that knowledge of reality is possible through the use of reason alone, i.e. without any resort to sense experience, and Descartes is certainly a 'rationalist' in this sense. However, since this definition of the word is not very useful and the word has a host of meanings that do not apply to Descartes (see above, pp.24, 31 and 71), I have avoided it as far as possible.

Scholasticism   Scholastic philosophy (and theology) was that

	taught in universities and colleges in Descartes's day (see above, *Aristotelianism*).
Stoicism	Descartes's ethical thought was influenced by the Christian Neo-Stoicism of his day which adopted and adapted the austere ethic of ancient Stoicism, one that extolled the supremacy of the will over passion and adverse circumstances.
Syllogism	A form of deductive reasoning containing two premises and a conclusion. A simple syllogism that will illustrate Descartes's basic criticisms of this form is:

    (1)   All men are immortal
    (2)   Socrates is a man
    (3)   Therefore Socrates is immortal

Since (3) is implicit in, 'contained' in (1) and (2), no 'new' truth has been discovered. In fact, of course, *empirically* (see above) (1) is false, (2) is true and (3) is false. Yet the syllogism is logically valid.

Tautology	A statement which must be true because of the meaning of its terms, e.g., 'all spinsters are unmarried'.
Teleology	The doctrine of *final causes* (see above), the view that developments are due to the purpose or design that is served by them (*O.E.D.*).
Theodicy	The vindication of divine providence in view of the existence of evil (*O.E.D.*).

Bibliographical Note

This is a small selection from the prodigious number of works on Descartes and seventeenth-century thought. Works asterisked are particularly recommended and, amongst these, *50* and *55* could be read first. Works double asterisked were of special help to me in writing this book, and works marked (B) contain useful bibliographical information.

A   Descartes's works

1   Adam, C., and Tannery, P., *Œuvres de Descartes* (Paris, Cerf, 1897-1913).

2   Cottingham, J., *Descartes's Conversation with Burman* (Oxford, Clarendon Press, 1976). This contains a useful introduction and notes.

B   On the Discours *or aspects thereof*

3   Chauvois, L., *Descartes, sa méthode et ses erreurs en physiologie*, préface de Jean Rostand (Paris, Editions du Cèdre, 1966). Chauvois examines Part 5 of the *Discours*, comparing Descartes's work in physiology unfavourably with Harvey's.

4   Denissoff, E., *Descartes, premier théoricien de la physique mathématique: trois essais sur le 'Discours de la Méthode'* (Paris, Editions Béatrice-Nauwelaerts, 1970). A vigorous defence of Cartesian science and a development of Gadoffre's historical reconstruction (see below, *6*) of the genesis of the *Discours*. In both domains he goes too far however.

5   Dijksterhuis, E.J., 'La Méthode et les Essais de Descartes', in *Descartes et le cartésianisme hollandais*, E.J. Dijksterhuis, C. Serrurier, P. Dibon et al. (Paris, P.U.F., 1950), pp.21-44. A useful discussion of the purpose and range of Part 2's four rules.

6**   Gadoffre, G., 'Introduction historique' to his edition of the *Discours de la Méthode* (Manchester, M.U.P., 1961). A brilliant historical reconstruction of the evolution of the *Discours*.

7**   Gilson, E., *'Discours de la Méthode', texte et commentaire* (Paris, Vrin, 1930). The indispensable tool for the student of the *Discours* and a monument to French scholarship little eroded by time.

8**   Gouhier, H., *Essais sur le 'Discours de la Méthode', la métaphysique et la morale* (Paris, Vrin, 1973). Excellent throughout but especially useful on the vexed question of the historicity of the *Discours*.

9**   Keefe, T., 'Descartes's 'morale provisoire': a reconsideration', in

French Studies, XXVI (2, April 1972), pp.129-42. A lucid and seminal critique of certain aspects of *6*.

10 Roth, H.L., *Descartes's 'Discourse on Method'* (Oxford, Clarendon Press, 1937). Now somewhat outdated, especially in its attitude to Cartesian science.

C *On other works by Descartes: on aspects of his thought: on Descartes's thought and/or life as a whole: on the bibliography of works on Descartes*

11 Alquié, F., *Descartes* (Paris, Hatier, 1956). An introduction to Descartes's life and work.

12* —— *La Découverte métaphysique de l'homme chez Descartes* (Paris, P.U.F., 1950). An essential work with distinctive views on the evolution of Descartes's metaphysical thinking.

13 Baillet, A., *La Vie de Monsieur Descartes*, 2 vols (Paris, 1691, Geneva, Slatkine Reprints, 1970). A somewhat idealised biography, not always reliable in its details, but full of interesting information.

14** Beck, L.J., *The Method of Descartes: a Study of the 'Regulae'* (Oxford, Clarendon Press, 1952). An invaluable work which throws much light on the *Discours*'s four rules and account of Descartes's scientific method.

15** —— *The Metaphysics of Descartes: a Study of the 'Méditations'* (Oxford, Clarendon Press, 1965). Another essential work, that elucidates the *Discours*'s somewhat obscure account of Descartes's metaphysics.

16 Brunschvicg, L., *Descartes et Pascal lecteurs de Montaigne* (New York, Brentano, 1944). See, especially, pp.113-54 for Descartes's debt to Montaigne.

17 Butler, R.J., ed., *Cartesian Studies* (Oxford, Blackwell, 1972). Stimulating essays by A. Kenny (see below, *27*) and others.

18(B) Doney, W., ed., *Descartes: a Collection of Critical Essays* (Garden City, New York, Doubleday, 1967). The useful bibliography is of books in English relating to Descartes.

19(B) —— 'Some recent work on Descartes: a bibliography', in *Philosophy Research Archives*, II, 1976.

20 Gaukroger, S., ed., *Descartes: Philosophy, Mathematics and Physics* (Sussex, Harvester Press, 1980). Essays by M. Gueroult (see below, *23*) and others which explore Descartes's attempt to provide a philosophical foundation for a mathematical physics.

21 Gouhier, H., *Les Premières Pensées de Descartes: contribution à l'histoire de l'anti-renaissance* (Paris, Vrin, 1958). How Descartes became a 'Cartesian'. Gouhier's study fills in many of the *Discours*'s gaps.

22* —— *La Pensée religieuse de Descartes* (Paris, Vrin, 1924). An illuminating study, by a great Descartes scholar, of an aspect of Descartes's thought ever-present in the *Discours*.

88 *Discours de la Méthode*

23** Gueroult, M., *Descartes selon l'ordre des raisons*, I: *L'Ame et Dieu*, II: *L'Ame et le corps* (Paris, Aubier, 1953). The most brilliant work on Descartes's metaphysics, demanding and therefore highly rewarding.

24(B) Hooker, M., ed., *Descartes: Critical and Interpretative Essays* (Baltimore and London, Johns Hopkins University Press, 1978). The bibliography by W. Doney (see above, *18* and *19*) is of some recent work on Descartes.

25* Keeling, S.V., *Descartes* (London, Benn, 1968). A standard work. Keeling's analysis brings out the strengths, the weaknesses and the importance of Descartes's philosophy.

26 Kemp Smith, N., *New Studies in the Philosophy of Descartes: Descartes as Pioneer* (London, Macmillan, 1952). A stimulating work on different aspects of Descartes's thought and life. See, especially, Chapters 2 and 3 on the Method and 13 on 'Descartes as pioneer'.

27* Kenny, A.J.P., *Descartes, a Study of his Philosophy* (New York, Random House, 1968). An invigorating book for the student of philosophy.

28** Laporte, J., *Le Rationalisme de Descartes* (Paris, P.U.F., 1945). An outstanding work, profound and clear, that questions, and rightly so in my view, the *idée reçue* that Descartes is a 'rationalist' (see above, p.84 under *Rationalism*).

29* Lefèvre, R., *L'Humanisme de Descartes* (Paris, P.U.F., 1957). A brilliant study of the Christian humanism of which the *Discours* is an expression.

30 —— *La Métaphysique de Descartes* (Paris, P.U.F., 1972). A good short introduction.

31 Milhaud, G., *Descartes savant* (Paris, Alcan, 1921). Milhaud's severe criticisms of Descartes's science are still worthy of consideration.

32 Ree, J., *Descartes* (London, Allen Lane, 1974). An interesting study, especially for its defence of Cartesian science.

33 Rodis-Lewis, G., *La Morale de Descartes* (Paris, P.U.F., 1957). An eloquent argument for the importance of ethics in Descartes's thought by a leading Descartes scholar.

34(B) —— *L'Œuvre de Descartes*, 2 vols (Paris, Vrin, 1971). An essential
** overview with valuable bibliographical indications.

35 Schouls, P.A., *The Imposition of Method: a Study of Descartes and Locke* (Oxford, Clarendon Press, 1980). An interesting account of the novelty of seventeenth-century thought.

36 Scott, J.F., *The Scientific Work of René Descartes* (London, Taylor and Francis, 1952). A balanced account of the scientific worth of the *Discours* and its *essais*.

37(B)* Sebba, G., *Bibliographia Cartesiana: a Critical Guide to the Descartes Literature 1800-1960* (The Hague, Nijhoff, 1964). An essential research tool.

38 Vrooman, J.R., *René Descartes: a Biography* (New York, Putnam,

1970). A useful, if sometimes speculative, introduction, rich in
background information.

39   Williams, B., *Descartes: the Project of Pure Enquiry* (London,
Penguin Books, 1978). A work for students of philosophy.

D   *On the background to Descartes's thought, general works that insert
Descartes's thought in a broader intellectual and/or social context*

40*   Barbour, I.G., *Issues in Science and Religion* (London, S.C.M. Press,
1966). Contains a clear account of the implications for Christian faith
of the seventeenth-century Scientific Revolution.

41*   Bréhier, E., *The History of Philosophy*, I: *The Seventeenth Century*,
translated by W. Baskin (Chicago and London, University of Chicago
Press, 1966). See Chapter 1 for an introduction to the seventeenth
century and Chapter 3 for a lucid introduction to Descartes's thought.

42(B)* Briggs, R., *The Scientific Revolution of the Seventeenth Century*
(London: Longmans, 1969). A good basic introduction, containing
useful background information and a bibliography.

43   Burtt, E.A., *The Metaphysical Foundations of Modern Science*
(London, Kegan Paul, Trench, 1925). A classic.

44   Chevalier, J., *Histoire de la pensée*, III: *La Pensée moderne: de
Descartes à Kant* (Paris, Flammarion, 1961). Good on Descartes the
Catholic metaphysician, little on Descartes's scientific thought.

45   Copleston, F., *History of Philosophy*, IV: *Descartes to Leibnitz*
(London, Burns & Oates, 1947-75). See Chapter 1 on the novelty of
seventeenth-century philosophy as well as Chapter 2 on Descartes.

46*   Dijksterhuis, E.J., *The Mechanisation of the World Picture*, translated
by C. Dikshoorn (Oxford, Clarendon Press, 1961). An essential work
on the seventeeth-century Scientific Revolution.

47   Dugas, R., *La Mécanique au XVIIe siècle: des antécédents scolastiques
à la pensée classique* (Neuchâtel, Editions du Griffon, 1954). Contains
a fair-minded evaluation of Descartes's science in its historical
background.

48*   Flew, A., *An Introduction to Western Philosophy: Ideas and
Argument from Plato to Sartre* (London, Thames and Hudson, 1971).
An introduction intended for philosophy students but useful for all.
See, especially, Chapters 8 to 11 on Descartes's metaphysics and
science.

49**   France, P., *Rhetoric and Truth in France: Descartes to Diderot*
(Oxford, Clarendon Press, 1972). Includes a useful examination of an
important yet neglected aspect of Descartes's work, its persuasive
function.

50*   Kearns, E.J., *Ideas in Seventeenth-Century France: the Most
Important Thinkers and the Climate of Ideas in Which They Worked*
(Manchester, M.U.P., 1979). A very useful introduction.

51*   Koyré, A., *From the Closed World to the Infinite Universe* (Baltimore,

Johns Hopkins Press, 1957). An essential study of the Scientific
Revolution showing how a philosopher's God and his world are
correlated.

52   —— *Newtonian Studies* (Harvard, University Press, 1965). See,
especially, Chapter 3 on Descartes and Newton.

53   Lenoble, R., *Mersenne ou la naissance du mécanisme* (Paris, Vrin,
1943). Mersenne, a Churchman, was a major correspondent of
Descartes, and encouraged him in his innovation (see above, p.12).

54   Popkin, R.H., *The History of Scepticism from Erasmus to Descartes*
(Assen, Van Gorcum, 1960). An interesting study, though the optic
chosen leads to an overplaying of the anti-sceptical motivation of
Descartes's thought. ·

55*   Potts, D.C., and D.G. Charlton, *French Thought since 1600* (London,
Methuen, 1974). A useful basic introduction.

56   Redwood, J., ed., *European Science in the Seventeenth Century*
(Newton Abbot, David and Charles, 1977). Contains illuminating texts
and documents.

57   Smith, A.G.R., *Science and Society in the Sixteenth and
Seventeenth Centuries* (London, Thames and Hudson, 1972). An
interesting discussion of the origins and nature of the seventeenth-
century Scientific Revolution and of its social effects.

58   Von Leyden, W., *Seventeenth-Century Metaphysics: an Examination
of Some Main Concepts and Theories* (London, Duckworth, 1968). A
lucid contribution to the history of philosophy and especially useful on
doubt (Part II) and the *cogito* (Part III).

59*   Whitehead, A.N., *Science and the Modern World* (Cambridge, C.U.P.,
1929). A classic. A critique of the seventeenth-century origins of
modern thought by a man who, like Descartes, was a great
mathematician and philosopher.

E   *Introduction to philosophy: for readers who wish to explore this
subject I suggest one or more of the following works*

60   Ewing, A.C., *The Fundamental Questions of Philosophy* (London,
Routledge and Kegan Paul, 1951).

61   Körner, S., *What is Philosophy? One Philosopher's Answer* (London,
Allen Lane, 1969).

62*   Lindley, R., ed., *What Philosophy Does* (London, Open Books, 1978).
A good basic introduction. The chapters on the philosophy of mind
and the philosophy of science are particularly useful to students of
Descartes.

63   Rosenberg, J.F., *The Practice of Philosophy: a Handbook for
Beginners* (Englewood Cliffs, New Jersey, Prentice-Hall, 1978).

64   Sprague, E., *What is Philosophy? a Short Introduction* (New York,
Oxford University Press, 1961).

CRITICAL GUIDES TO FRENCH TEXTS

edited by

Roger Little, Wolfgang van Emden, David Williams